WORKING
WITH
ARCHANGELS

WORKING
WITH
ARCHANGELS

A path to transformation and power

Theolyn Cortens

PIATKUS

First published in Great Britain in 2007 by
Piatkus Books Ltd
5 Windmill Street, London W1T 2JA
email: info@piatkus.co.uk

The moral right of the author has been asserted

A catalogue record for this book is available from the British Library

ISBN 978 0 7499 2800 1

Edited by Anthea Courtenay
Copy-edited by Krystyna Mayer
Diagrams by Will Shaman

This book has been printed on paper manufactured with respect for the environment using wood from managed sustainable resources

Typeset by Palimpsest Book Production Limited,
Grangemouth, Stirlingshire
Printed and bound in Great Britain by
William Clowes Ltd, Beccles, Suffolk

Dedicated to the memory of

Ray Cortens

1922–80

It matters not how strait the gate,
How charged with punishments the scroll,
I am the master of my fate:
I am the captain of my soul.

W. E. HENLEY

Contents

Acknowledgements

I would like to thank the following:

Anthea Courtenay for being a patient and meticulous editor, without whom this book could not have been finished.

Will Shaman for being a dear companion on my spiritual journey – and for supplying the diagrams.

Anne Hill for talking to me about her experiences with 'the Lady' and for allowing me to use her story and quote from her poem.

Rosemary Ellen Guiley for allowing me to use the story of Juliet's encounter with Michael, from Rosemary's book *Angels of Mercy*.

Kathleen Pepper for discussing essences and archangels, and for sharing her Sandalphon story.

Maureen Lockhart for allowing me to use her Sandalphon story.

The Alister Hardy Trust for permission to quote from the archive of spiritual experiences held at the University of Wales, Lampeter.

Also a special thank you to my students and SoulSchool teachers for contributing their stories.

And last but not least, thank you to the archangels – especially Raziel!

Theolyn, London, 2007

Vision

(written a few days before the experience described in the Introduction)

Last night I woke
And saw an angel
Seated on my bed.
In starched white linen,
With alabaster hands
And gleaming feathers
On molten, golden wings.
A face of such stern gentleness
As carved in Florence marble
And surrounded by a nimbus
Of such light as human eyes
Could not gaze upon,
That overwhelmed the
Mechanics of my brain.

So motionless, so still,
It gazed with eyes
I feared to meet,
For it seemed that
Within their timeless orbs
I might lose all knowledge of myself.

Theolyn Cortens

Introduction

And it came to pass . . . that the heavens were opened and
a blinding light of exceptional brilliance flowed through my
entire brain. And so it kindled my whole heart and breast
like a flame, not burning but warming . . . and suddenly I
understood the meaning of expositions of the books . . .
HILDEGARDE OF BINGEN

Over 30 years ago I had an awe-inspiring experience that was to
change my life. I was lying ill in bed, meditating, when I heard
sweet voices telling me I would meet my God. I immediately
wondered if I was going to die – though I only had mumps! I had
no sense of fear; I just lay back in complete surrender to the
inevitable. Almost immediately I was surrounded by a brilliant light,
brighter than sunshine, which filled my whole body with warmth,
power and energy. As the light embraced me I asked in my mind,
'Are you Gabriel?' There was no reply.

I don't know how long the light was with me, but when I sat up
and swung my legs over the bed, my mind was in turmoil – part
of me wondering at the beauty and delight of the experience, part of
me trying to decide what exactly had happened. Although the voices
had told me it was God I was about to meet, somehow I had the
impression that this was an angel. At the time I wondered whether
this visitation meant that I was supposed to take up a spiritual voca-
tion, an idea that made me very nervous indeed. I was a single
mother with two children, working in my first teaching job: I couldn't
see myself preaching to people about the kingdom of God. Anyway,

1

even if I had encountered a messenger from God, it was far from clear what the message was.

The experience stayed with me. I spent the next few weeks in a state of bliss and received many inner messages from the sweet voices – one of which was that I would meet someone I would marry. This state of consciousness was very beautiful, and opened my eyes to the magic and glory of Creation. I experienced the underlying unity of all apparently separate things, and understood how everything that happens fits into a perfect pattern. However, in this state it was impossible to live an ordinary life, and eventually I asked to be 'brought back to Earth'. I had a sense of sadness about this, but shortly afterwards I met Will, the man to whom I have now been married for 32 years, and a new joy came into my life.

A few years later I went to live in Somerset, near Glastonbury, where I had another powerful experience. One summer afternoon in 1982, I was walking my baby in her pushchair down a country lane, when I felt the presence of a majestic being hanging in the air between heaven and Earth, its feet on the rolling landscape, its head in the heavens. I didn't 'see' this being, but when I was meditating the next day I was surprised by an inner vision that appeared suddenly in my mind, like a picture on a cinema screen. The image was of an angel walking in the English countryside. The angel's head, surrounded by a vast halo of radiant light, reached far into the heavens. As I gazed at him I noticed some interesting details. He was wearing a white gown that shone as though it was made of some unearthly material. In one hand he carried an olive branch, in the other a large blue crystal. On his feet he wore plain brown sandals and in the landscape behind him, on the top of a hill, was a shining building that looked like some kind of temple. Behind him skipped a lamb, tiny beside his vast height.

Although I had been meditating for several years I had never had such a powerful vision. Sometimes during meditation I would receive words and phrases that developed into poems, but I never expected to receive such a clear visual image. I decided to paint what I had seen. I couldn't hope to capture the real essence of this tall presence, but I wanted to keep a record of the details, so I found a large sheet of paper and did my best. Although the result isn't a good painting I have kept it all these years, and whenever I look at it I recall the intensity of the vision and how it affected me a quarter of a century ago.

In the 1980s there were no Mind, Body and Spirit sections in bookshops, with a ready supply of books on angels. So I didn't go looking for information about this angel, and I didn't talk to anyone about it – except my husband Will. To me, this was just a beautiful angel who had paid me a personal visit because I was meditating, and I didn't expect anyone else to be interested. However, a few months later I came across an art book in the library – *Angels* by Peter Lamborn Wilson – which examined ideas about angels and other winged beings throughout history. As I flicked through the pages I came across a reproduction of a woodcut dated 1516 showing a bearded man in Renaissance clothes. The man is seated in a room, his hand outstretched to grasp the lower section of a curious diagram – one that was to become very familiar to me in the following years. (I discuss this further in the chapter on working with archangels, and you will find a version of the diagram on p. 38.)

What it showed was a series of circles joined by lines – I thought it looked a little like the map of the London Underground. The text explained that this was indeed a map, a spiritual map called the Tree of Life, created many centuries ago by Jewish mystics who meditated according to a system called Kabbalah,[1] in order to gain insights into the mysteries of life. These mystics, called 'kabbalists', seemed to have an intimate knowledge of angels.

Fascinated, I read on – and I was well rewarded. The book explained that the Tree of Life demonstrates the flow of divine energy throughout Creation. Each of the ten circles on the Tree of Life represents a container of this creative energy called a *sefira* (the plural is *sefirot*), and each *sefira* has one or two archangels as its guardian. Peter Lamborn Wilson describes the tree as 'like a rose bush on which ten measureless blossoms of light appear . . . each of the roses of light will unfold its petals and reveal a winged figure'. (Rather more appealing than a Tube map!)

Each *sefira* represents a different attribute of God, and each has an individual name, as do the archangels. The *sefira* at the bottom of the Tree, I learned, is called the Kingdom, and the archangel who guards the Kingdom is Sandalphon. I felt a rush of excitement – my angel had been wearing sandals and he certainly seemed to be walking in a beautiful natural kingdom. In his hand he held a blue crystal, and I was fascinated to discover that the Hebrew word *sefira* has a connection with sapphires and crystals in general.

The book mentioned some other archangels by name. Some of them I had heard of, like Michael and Gabriel, while others were new to me, such as Samael and Zaphkiel. Wanting to know more, I began to search for information about the Tree of Life from other sources. When I realised that the Kabbalah is a very complex subject with many deep philosophical theories about the Creation, I decided to go to books that would give me the basics – like the names of the *sefirot* and the archangels – and to ask for any further information to come to me during meditation. After all, I thought, Sandalphon appeared without even being asked: perhaps I could ask other archangels to show themselves on my inner cinema screen.

Over the next few months I meditated on the names of the Archangels of the Tree of Life. I imagined the Tree as a tall block of flats with lifts to different floors. I would visualise going up in a lift to a particular floor, where I would ask the doors to open to reveal the archangel who 'lived' there. While waiting for the lift doors to open I often had the impression that I was opening a gateway into a dimension of light. Later I discovered that these archangels are sometimes called 'the Guardians of the Gates of Light'.

Sometimes the vision would come immediately; sometimes I might meditate for weeks before the next archangel would appear. It took ages to meet Gabriel. When I asked to meet him during meditation, I kept seeing images like those in Renaissance paintings or on Victorian Christmas cards, often showing Gabriel with the Virgin Mary. This made me very aware of the difference between an imaginative inner picture, created from my previous cultural knowledge, and a genuine vision that would arise in my mind from a deep place of spiritual knowing. Throughout, I kept a personal journal, but I never imagined I would share my visions with anyone else.

When I started to work with the archangels in the 1980s, I found I was gradually becoming more aware of their presence even when I wasn't meditating. I realised that it was important for me to write down my insights about the archangels, and in 1991 I began to organise all my notes. At that time no publishers wanted books on angels. So, with my husband Will's help, *Discovering Angels* was self-published in 1996, 22 years after the original 'visitation' during my illness. I began to talk to people about the book, and then found myself offering one-day workshops, so that I could demonstrate the visualisation techniques I had developed for myself, and help other people to meet the archangels. By the late 1990s it was clear that there was a growing interest in angels, and in 2000 I started SoulSchool, offering courses enabling people to work with the archangels at home. A couple of years later, Piatkus commissioned me to write *Living with Angels*. Now you can use this book to start your own journey with the archangels.

Times have really changed since my first encounters. In recent years angels have become ever more popular with spiritual seekers. Today there are numerous books on the subject, and a number of spiritual teachers are helping people who want to make contact with angels. We no longer believe that they live in realms impossible for us to reach, but understand that they are close at hand, co-creating the world we live in. Many people are reporting first-hand experiences of help and comfort from angelic beings, often during times of illness or bereavement. Participants in my workshops who make contact with their Guardian Angels often say that they will never feel alone again.

Perhaps you are already working with angels to bring more joy and peace into your daily life. You may have read my earlier books, *Living with Angels* and *Working with Your Guardian Angel*. Or maybe you are quite new to the powerful idea that every human being can work with the angels to co-create happiness and abundance for themselves and to encourage peace and joy in the world. Whatever stage you have reached on your spiritual journey, this book will guide you through the angelic realms; you will learn how to contact your Guardian Angel, who will support you as you commune with the great creative powers we call the archangels.

There are many, many archangels in Creation, but you will find that the most powerful helpers in your personal life are the Archangels of the Tree of Life and the archangel of your own zodiac Sun sign. By the time you have read this book and experienced all the inner journeys described here, you will have gained confidence and a sense of empowerment. You will be ready to move into your chosen destiny.

PART 1

Who are the Archangels?

About this book

You are about to embark on an exciting spiritual journey, in which you will be taken to meet and work with archangels. Whether or not you are already working with angels, you will probably know that archangels are usually considered higher in rank than ordinary angels. However, to have a meaningful relationship with the archangels, you need a really clear idea about who they are and what they do. In order to explain this I want to take you right back to the beginning of Creation.

Most scientists explain the birth of the universe in terms of an event known as the Big Bang, a vast explosion in space out of which, after many millions of years, today's universe evolved. Most religions use different terminology to tell the same story. According to these stories, the universe began when a divine being, or God, decided to create everything we know, using intention, will and power to get the process started. The Creator's original intention unfolded through a series of stages until the universe as we know it was manifested, and celestial helpers were created to support the process. Most religions speak of invisible forces that help to create and uphold the universe. In some religions they are called gods and goddesses, but in the Judaic, Christian and Islamic traditions they are described as angelic or celestial beings.

Celestial beings

Each group of celestial beings has a particular role to play in Creation. Let us take a brief look at the place of the archangels in the celestial realms.

The Seraphim

The Seraphim are the closest beings to God. The Bible describes them as having six wings each and they blaze with fiery light (the Hebrew word *serap* means to burn). The prophet Isaiah saw them in the Temple, surrounding the divine throne, and heard them singing *'Kadosh, Kadosh, Kadosh'*, which means 'Holy, Holy, Holy' (Isaiah 6.1–8). This beautiful refrain, witnessed by a prophet 2,800 years ago, is still sung in Jewish and Christian liturgy around the world. In the Catholic Church it is sung in Latin – *'Sanctus, Sanctus, Sanctus'*. Isaiah's vision shows us that the beings closest to the divine power are full of passion and delight, encouraging the creative process by constantly affirming its holiness. I like to think of the seraphim as divine cheerleaders, activating and sustaining the energy required for Creation.

The Archangels

Archangels are airy beings who take charge of the hidden structures of Creation. They are organisers and planners: they can be likened to the architects of the universe, sorting out the plans, working out where the joists and pillars should be placed, and organising the necessary fixtures and fittings. Each is in charge of a particular area, dealing with a different aspect of Creation. Each has a special quality, which it can help human beings to develop. For example, Archangel Michael can help us develop courage, while the healing Archangel Raphael helps us develop empathy.

The Angels

There are countless numbers of angels – according to Jewish tradition new angels are being created every day. Their loving work is to weave the delicate tapestry of Creation from moment to moment. Having once worked as a dress designer, I often think that the angels are like the stitches that keep a garment together. The loving power of the Divine maintains Creation constantly, and the angels are always present – even if we don't notice them. One of their tasks is to help us to relate to each other: they bring emotional balance, harmony and love into our lives.

Nature Spirits

In the world of nature spirits you will find fairies, elves and other elementals. These spirits are very practical. They maintain the visible fabric of our planet, caring for every blade of grass, every flower and every creature, great or small. It is our world that they care for, and we too should be working as stewards to protect and maintain the kingdom of Earth.

The Cherubim

Over-arching all these four realms are the mighty cherubim, described by the prophet Ezekiel (Ezekiel 1.1–28) as fierce creatures, shining like burnished bronze, with four faces that relate to the elements: a lion (Leo/Fire), a man (Aquarius/Air), an eagle (an old representation for Scorpio/Water) and an ox (Taurus/Earth). Over the years the cherubim have been demoted by artists to plump little babies with tiny wings. In fact, we should envisage them as huge beings of light spreading their wings over all four aspects of Creation, protecting and holding Creation throughout time.

The Four Worlds

The four realms of angels correspond well with the four-stage model for the creative process found in Greek philosophy, which relates each stage to one of the four elements.

Seraphim	Fire: passionate intent – beginning the process
Archangels	Air: developing the idea – maintaining the intent
Angels	Water: nurturing Creation – cooling and forming
Nature spirits	Earth: activating form – manifestation

The Greeks also talked about a fifth element, called the *Quinta Essentia* (the fifth essence) or *Anima Mundi* (the Spirit of the World). This element is like glue, holding everything together, much like the cherubim.

The Archangels

In this book you will meet some of the many, many archangels who support Creation and help humanity develop to its highest possibility. The archangels, like the angels, have no gender since they don't have physical bodies, but some have gentle, soft qualities that make them more 'feminine', while others are more challenging and appear more 'masculine'. In this book I refer to them as 'he' or 'she' partly according to tradition (Michael, for example, is always thought of as male), and partly according to my own experience and accounts gathered from other people.

I recount some of the stories that have gathered around the archangels over the centuries, and describe my own visions and those of my students and colleagues. You will also be given practical suggestions for ways to work with the archangels in your everyday life.

The origins of the Archangels

In ancient texts, including the Bible, archangels traditionally have individual names – unlike angels. Knowing the names of the archangels is the first step to developing a powerful relationship with them. As we will see, their names indicate their qualities and the roles they play in Creation. Sometimes we find that a particular archangel has taken on a major role in the development of a religious tradition – Gabriel, for example, is a key character in the story of the birth of Jesus and therefore of Christianity, and he also brought the Koran to the Prophet Mahomet and thus helped to found Islam. Some archangels are less well known and we have to search for clues, or rely on less well-known stories and visions, in order to get in touch with their qualities and tune in to their energies.

Our information about the angelic realms comes down to us mainly from the ancient Jewish tradition, which was influenced by even earlier religious ideas. This is why, with only one or two exceptions, the archangels have Hebrew names. The first part of the name describes the quality of the archangel, the second part – 'el' – means 'of God'. For example, in the name 'Raphael', *raph* is Hebrew for healing, so Raphael's name means 'healing of God'.

Over the centuries, stories and ideas about archangels have been added to the original Hebrew stories by both Christians and Muslims, and more recently by New Age teachers who link some of them to the chakras – the energy centres of the human body according to yogic tradition. In this book I offer material based on the older traditions, which I have found to be very powerful, together with my own direct experiences.

The four chief Archangels

The best-known archangels are the ones who appear in the Hebrew Bible and the Apocrypha: Michael (like unto God), Gabriel (strength of God), Raphael (healing of God) and Auriel (often spelt Uriel – light of God). These four archangels often appear in stained glass windows in Christian churches, and are famous for their roles in upholding the four corners of the world and governing the elements. Ancient star gazers noticed four especially bright stars in the sky which they called the Four Watchers, and later Christian and Jewish astronomers identified these Watchers with the four archangels. As the history of star lore is over 5,000 years old, you can imagine that various opinions have arisen over the centuries about which archangel should be associated with which direction and which star, and in my research I have discovered many competing versions.

Traditionally, the archangels do not have fixed placements relating to planet Earth, and cannot be identified with any specific point of the compass or any particular geographical location. In *Living With Angels* I offered the following as my favourite line-up of archangels for the four directions, and you may like to adopt it:

Michael – South
Gabriel – West
Raphael – East
Auriel (Uriel) – North

These four archangels are also included in a very special group of twelve archangels that you are going to meet in this book. These are the Archangels of the Tree of Life, sometimes called the Guardians of the Gates of Light.

Using this book

The best way to use this book is to treat Part 2 as a road map, a guide to a journey. You will then meet each archangel in order on the Tree of Life, starting from the foot of the Tree. In this way you will experience the archangels' various qualities in your life and will be able to call on any of them to assist you in any situation – from sitting an examination to asking for a pay rise.

In Part 3 you will find information about another group of twelve archangels – the Archangels of the Zodiac Signs. I suggest ways in which you can work with the archangel of your own sign, and how you can ask any of the twelve for help in developing your latent possibilities.

Working with archangels creates an opening to other dimensions of your being. This process allows you to repair difficult relationships, heal old emotional wounds, awaken your spiritual wisdom and lay the groundwork for an exciting new chapter in your life. By the time you have read this book, you will be able to choose a Dream Team of celestial supporters. Before embarking on this inspiring journey, let me tell you more about the archangels – about who they are and what they do.

The Archangels through history

How manifold are thy works! They are hidden from before us, O thou sole god, whose power no other possesses.
PHARAOH AKHENATON'S HYMN TO THE GOD ATON

Shamans and Spirits

To understand the history of the archangels, we need to know some-thing of how humanity's ideas about God developed. Anthropologists tell us that early in human history, many thousands of years ago, spiritual practitioners attempted to communicate with the invisible forces supporting the natural world. Like their descendants today, known in some cultures as shamans, they believed that events were influenced by spirits. They developed techniques that enabled them to journey to other worlds and bring back knowledge which would help their tribes. Their visions inspired paintings and carvings, which were used to help them manifest positive results in their day-to-day world. Gradually these practices led to the worship of specific gods and goddesses – the god of rain, the goddess of harvest and so on. Each tribe worshipped its own god, as well as gods who had universal powers over the natural world.

The Babylonian Gods

While the human race was divided into many tribes, there were many gods. But as individual rulers began taking power over large territories, concepts about the gods also changed, and the idea of a chief god began to emerge.

In ancient Mesopotamia, around 4,000 years ago, the god Marduk was the patron deity of the city of Babylon. The Babylonians had a number of other gods, but gradually Marduk was credited with the qualities of a ruler, and became chief of the gods. In the Babylonian Creation myth *Enuma Elish*, Marduk sets the stars in the heavens as homes for the great gods; he fixes the cycle of the zodiac and divides the year into twelve months. Marduk is associated with the Sun and is described as the creator of grains and plants 'who caused the green herb to spring up'. Clearly, there are many similarities between this Creation myth and the story of God's creation of the world in the biblical Book of Genesis.

Aton, the Egyptian God

As theories about the supernatural became more sophisticated an idea developed that would change human history and that still affects the world today – the belief that there is only one God, the God who created and sustains the whole universe.

At about the time when the Babylonians were developing their Sun god myth, the Egyptians were worshipping Amun-Re, the Sun god, along with many other deities. In the twelfth century BC the Pharaoh Akhenaton, known as 'The Father of Monotheism', attempted to steer the Egyptians away from their many minor gods to worship Aton as the one and only god. Akhenaton called this one god 'the Divine Light which is in the Sun disc, living eternally and forever'. The Egyptian priests resisted this new idea, which threatened their power and livelihood, and Akhenaton became very unpopular. In around 1353 BC he left the city of Thebes and created a new city in honour of Aton, Akhetaten (now called Amarna), together with his wife Nefertiti. Their son, the famous boy pharaoh Tutankhamen, was probably born and crowned there. After Akhenaton's death his new city was destroyed by jealous factions.

Ahura Mazda and the Bounteous Immortals

Another important figure who promoted the worship of the Sun was Zarathustra, or Zoroaster, whose religious ideas influenced Middle Eastern society for thousands of years. Zoroaster's dates are difficult to pin down but many scholars believe he may have lived as early as 1200 BC. Zoroaster's writings, the *Gathas*, may be the oldest scriptures in the world. We do know that this early prophet had a major impact on religion in the Middle East with his idea of one God of Light, Ahura Mazda, and an equally powerful God of Darkness, Ahriman.

Zoroaster believed that Ahura Mazda had powerful assistants, called the *Amesha Spentas* – the Bounteous Immortals. The *Spentas* are all the divinities that help to strengthen and further Creation; like angels, they are benevolent helpers. (In the Hindu Vedas we find similar characters called *Vishve Amrtas*, the collective term for all supernatural beings – literally 'all immortals'.) Significantly for us, Zoroaster introduced the idea that the God of Light had six particular *Spentas*, divine sparks that are the first six emanations from the creative source whose task it is to manifest the universe. Each of these *Spentas* has a particular quality: good purpose, right-eousness, desirable dominion, holy devotion, wholeness and immortality. These are not only essential for building Creation, but are qualities that mortal beings should strive to possess. The doctrine of the great six is that through good thoughts, words and deeds, each individual should strive to emulate the *Amesha Spentas*. We can see why it is generally accepted by scholars that the *Spentas* are the original archangels.

Archangels and Judaism

The story of the archangels is closely tied to the history of Judaism. The earliest suggested date for the first Jewish patriarch, Abraham, is around 1800 BC. In the Book of Genesis Abraham is called by God to leave his home city of Ur and travel to Canaan, where, says God, Abraham will found a great nation (Genesis 12.1–2).

The Jewish people, then known as the Hebrews, suffered many tribulations, journeying for years before they settled in their own land. The patriarch Moses (1527–1407 BC) was brought up in the Egyptian court, where he may have been influenced by the ideas of Akhenaton. God instructed Moses to rescue his people and take them out of Egypt to a 'promised land'.

The Sons of God

In the 8th century BC the prophet Isaiah had a vision of the heavenly throne of God in the Temple (Isaiah 6.1–8), during which he saw the seraphim,[2] though he does not mention seeing the sons of God, or any particular angels. Another prophet, Ezekiel, who prophesied during the Jewish exile in Babylon, describes a vision of a sapphire throne and claims to have seen the 'glory of the Lord' surrounded by four angelic figures with many wings and faces – these were the cherubim.

Around 526 BC the Israelites were exiled in Babylon, where they were influenced by other religious traditions that had developed in the Middle East, including Zoroastrianism. Most scholars believe that this is when the Jewish people began to think about angels as God's helpers and messengers. In the Book of Job (Job 1.6)[3] we can read about God having a conversation with the *bene elohim*, the 'sons of God', who present themselves before God rather like counsellors reporting to a monarch: some scholars interpret these as angels.

Around the 5th century BC we find several encounters with archangels in the Book of Daniel. First, the prophet Daniel recounts the story of Shadrach, Meshach and Abednego, three Jewish captives who are thrown into a furnace for refusing to worship the Babylonian gods (Daniel 3). Mysteriously, a fourth figure, described as like the 'Son of God', appears in the fire with them, and all four are unharmed. Next Daniel relates how a 'watcher and a holy one came down from heaven' to help him interpret his dreams (Daniel 4.13). Later, Daniel hears a voice naming Gabriel and instructing the archangel to explain a vision to him (Daniel 8.16). In yet another vision

Archangel Michael tells Daniel that he will help deliver the Israelites from their enemies (Daniel 10.13). These are the first mentions of archangels by name in the Bible.

The Archangel Raphael is first named in the Book of Enoch (see below), and later in the Book of Tobit, as 'one of the seven angels who stand ready and enter before the glory of the Lord' (Tobit 12.15).[4] The last archangel of the 'famous four', Uriel (Auriel), is not mentioned until much later, in the Second Book of Esdras[5] in which Uriel is sent from heaven to answer the questions put to God by the prophet Ezra (2 Esdras 4.1–4).

Many more Archangels

Many stories about archangels are found in texts that have been excluded from both the Hebrew Bible and the Christian canon. One important text that tells us a great deal about named angels was only discovered by European scholars at the beginning of the 17th century. This is the Book of Enoch, said to have been written by the grandfather of Noah, who is mentioned in Genesis (Genesis 5.18). The Book of Enoch contains descriptions of Enoch's visionary journeys to heaven and was probably written down around 160 BC, though almost certainly belonging to a much older oral tradition.

Enoch presents us with the concept that there are not just four major archangels, but seven. Many subsequent teachings mention the Seven Archangels of the Presence, with differing lists of names. The most famous list was supplied in the 6th century by a mysterious Christian writer known as Pseudo-Dionysius.[6] It includes archangels called Zadkiel, Jophiel and Chamuel, as well as Michael, Raphael, Gabriel and Auriel. This version of the 'magnificent seven' is found in most contemporary angel books.

The Tree of Life

The idea of a tree representing the flow of divine energy through heaven and Earth is very old. If you visit the Assyrian section in the British Museum you can see carvings from the palace walls of Nineveh dating back nearly 3,000 years. Some of these show a winged man watering a tree with flowers evenly distributed on either side. Archaeologists believe this is an image of a sacred tree.

A version of the Tree of Life also appears in the philosophy of the Essenes, a spiritual group who lived in the desert, separated from the mainstream Jewish tradition of the Temple with its high priests. The famous ruins at Qumran, where the Dead Sea Scrolls were found in 1947, belonged to an Essene community. The Essene tradition is very ancient – nobody can say exactly how old it is – but the 1st-century Jewish writer Flavius Josephus (AD 37–100) reported that the Essenes were already established in the 2nd century BC and that their history went back to a 'remote age'.

The Essenes believed in seven heavenly angels or cosmic forces, balanced by seven earthly or terrestrial forces, so their Tree of Life showed fourteen angels of Creation. The Tree was pictured with seven roots reaching down into the earth and seven branches extending upwards, symbolising humanity's relationship to both Earth and heaven. The angels on the Essene Tree were referred to by their qualities or functions; for example, the Angel of Life, the Angel of Joy, the Angel of the Sun, the Angel of Water and the Angel of Air. The Book of Enoch was one of the texts found among the Dead Sea Scrolls, so the Essenes must have been familiar with Enoch's seven named archangels.

Jewish mysticism and the Tree of Life

The Jewish mystical tradition has always been very concerned with how Creation begins and how it is maintained, which is why their spiritual texts are such a rich source of information about the archangels. The visions of the prophets and the patriarchs are the earliest reports of mystical experiences in the *Tanakh* – the Hebrew Bible, known to Christians as the Old Testament – and, as we have seen, many of them included angels. The branch of Jewish mysticism known as Kabbalah, which uses the Tree of Life with its archangels as a model for the Creation, is reputed to be as old as

Abraham himself. Since Abraham may have lived as early as the 18th century BC, Kabbalah could be nearly 4,000 years old. Abraham was born in Ur, in southern Mesopotamia,[7] and lived in Egypt, so it is likely that he was familiar with early astrological knowledge and with the ancient Egyptian mysteries.

However, the earliest kabbalistic text, the *Sefer Yetzirah* – meaning 'Book of Creation' – was probably written down about 200–100 BC. This book explains how God uses a series of paths to channel the divine energy that manifests and sustains Creation. The flowing energy of the Divine through these paths is called *shefa*, which means 'everflow': you could think of it as the life force, *chi* or *prana*.[8] The linking points between the paths are called *sefirot* (in the plural) – a word that can be translated as 'containers' – and each *sefira* (singular) contains a divine quality or attribute. The pattern made by the paths and the containers is called the Tree of Life. (*See* Diagrams 1 and 2 in the next chapter, pages 38 and 39)

In the commentary to the *Sefer Yetzirah* we learn that God's providence works through the angels, while the angels in turn work through the stars and planets. We are also told that there are two kinds of angel: the angels that are created with every word of God on a daily basis, who sustain Creation, and the angels with names, like Gabriel and Michael, who have a permanent existence. According to another Jewish tradition, one angel cannot have two missions and two angels cannot share a mission; each angel has a specific role in Creation. The planets (only seven were known to the ancients) and the stars each have an angel or archangel.

Another notable kabbalistic book is the *Bahir* ('The Book of Illumination'), published in the 12th century, but possibly much older. The *Bahir* has much to tell us about the roles of the archangels, especially Michael, Gabriel and Auriel. The *Zohar* ('The Book of Splendour'), which was circulating in the 13th century, provides stories about Archangel Metatron and his 'bride', the Shekinah, as well as the four major archangels. The *Sha'are Ore* ('The Gates of Light') was written in the 13th century AD. In this mystical text, the 'gates' refer to the *sefirot*, and the archangels are sometimes called 'Guardians of the Gates of Light'.

Other stories about angels are found in ancient Jewish legends, most of which are impossible to date: there was a rich oral tradition long before these legends and folk tales were written down and collected. Accounts of mysterious events often involving angels and archangels can be found in a variety of Jewish texts, collectively known as the *Aggadah*. These texts provide us with a treasure trove of inspirational stories that I researched for my MA and for this book. In many of these tales, the angels are portrayed as rebellious, and jealous of humans.

Fallen Angels and the war in heaven

In some legends the angels' rebelliousness goes so far as to become a war in heaven, ending with the wicked angels being cast out. In the Book of Enoch, for example, the prophet describes how Michael, with the other archangels, relays to God complaints they have been receiving from the most saintly humans, asking that bad angels be expelled from Earth. In this version the Archangel Raphael throws the wicked angel Azazel into darkness until the Day of Judgement. Around the same time *The War of the Sons of Light against the Sons of Darkness*, found among the Dead Sea Scrolls, tells how the forces of light, led by Archangel Michael (described as a Prince of Light) defeat the battalions of Beliar,[9] the Prince of Darkness.

The idea that the one all-powerful God would create, or allow to exist, an almost equally powerful opponent bent on overthrowing him is paradoxical, but it has been perpetuated by Christian stories such as the battle in heaven found in the Book of Revelation. Revelation is a vivid account by St John the Divine (1st century AD) of his visions describing a period of extraordinary turmoil leading up to the second coming of Jesus and the complete transformation of the human race. Here St Michael and his angels fight a dragon, defeating him and his angels (Revelation 12.7–9).

In more recent times, the story of the prideful Lucifer (as the chief fallen angel was later named), who was ejected from heaven because of his disobedience to God, was popularised by the poet John Milton in *Paradise Lost* (1667). (The 'Devil' with horns and a tail is a medieval construct, whose image is based on the pagan god Pan.)

Stories of fallen angels come from a very old tradition which arose from the need to explain how evil came into the world. In these dualistic stories the forces of good and evil are in continual conflict. But older still is the holistic view that everything that happens on Earth, good or bad, is under God's jurisdiction. My view is that 'fallen angels' represent aspects of ourselves that we need to come to terms with.

Christianity and the Celestial Hierarchies

Jesus was Jewish, but very shortly after his death Christianity developed as a new faith. Angels appear several times in the Christian gospels; in particular, Gabriel appears to Mary to announce the coming of a new spiritual teacher (Luke 1.26). Christianity was spread throughout the Mediterranean by St Paul, who is regarded as the most important interpreter of Jesus's teachings. St Paul never met Jesus in person, and started out by persecuting Christians. After his blinding revelation on the road to Damascus (Acts 9.3), he was led to begin preaching Christianity. In his letters, St Paul specifically warns his flock not to be beguiled into worshipping angels (Colossians 2.18) and to seek salvation only through Jesus.

In the 6th century AD, Pseudo-Dionysius developed the famous mystical map of the Celestial Hierarchies. If you have read other books about angels you may be familiar with this diagram, which shows a series of nine concentric circles around the centre point, which is God. A variety of celestial beings inhabits these spheres. Some of the celestial beings have familiar names – cherubim, seraphim, archangels and angels. The 'thrones' may be derived from Ezekiel's famous chariot vision (Ezekiel 1.1–28), in which the cherubim surround the throne of God. In Hebrew there is a class of celestial being called the *Ophanim*, which means 'wheels', and Ezekiel mentions many wheels. However, the wheels and thrones do not seem to be angelic beings, just a means of celestial transport driven by the cherubim energy.

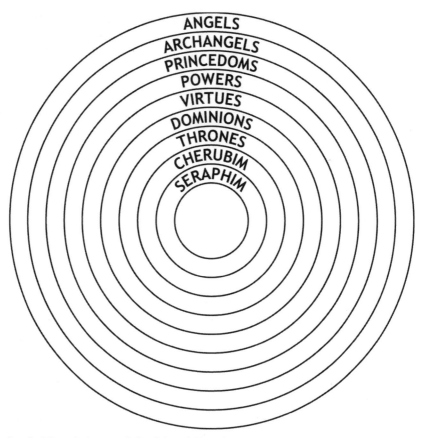

Pseudo-Dionysius's map of the Celestial Hierachies

Thrones, principalities, dominions and powers are all mentioned in St Paul's letters (Colossians 1.16), but many scholars believe that these refer to earthly rather than heavenly systems of government. Pseudo-Dionysius claimed to be St Paul's disciple (even though he lived 500 years after Paul), so he may have derived these names from Paul's letters. 'Virtues' represent qualities that humans are supposed to aspire to – for example, patience, hope and charity – and come from Greek mythology. They are depicted with wings in Greek statues, but they are not heavenly beings.

The Celestial Hierarchies were envisioned at a time when people still believed that the Earth was the centre of the universe with the planets revolving around it in a series of crystal spheres, one inside each other, like Russian dolls. God was thought of as like an all-powerful monarch, surrounded by ranks of servants of varying degrees of importance. Nowadays we can think of angels and archangels, whatever their task, as being networkers, interacting with each other on a much more democratic basis. I am sure that the angels are not interested in status: they just get on with what has to be done. Ishvara d'Angelo, who paints beautiful angels, refers to 'families' of angels and I find this idea much more appealing for today than hierarchies.

Although Pseudo-Dionysius was distrusted by some contemporary churchmen, his map of heavenly beings was gradually accepted by Christians. Despite St Paul's warnings, angels remained popular with most Christians, except among the Protestant groups who broke away from the Catholic Church during the Reformation in the 16th century. They emphasised direct communication with God and Jesus, so they were not interested in looking to angels or saints for help.

The Islamic religion, founded in the 6th century, also has a tradition of angels, which includes the Archangel Jibrael or Jibril (Gabriel) who brought the *Holy Koran* to the Prophet Mahomet. Islam developed in the Middle East and the angels of Islam have many similarities to those in the Jewish and Christian traditions.

Magicians and their rituals

During the Renaissance period, which began in the late 15th century, Christian philosophers and theologians became interested in ancient writings outside their own tradition. Many of them came to believe that Jewish mysticism could be reconciled with Christian ideas. Some of these European philosophers were fascinated by the idea that Kabbalah held the secrets of Creation, knowledge that would enable them to have an effect on the material world. Known as alchemists, they were especially keen to transmute base metal into gold and used rituals to summon angels in order to become effective magicians.

Famous alchemists like Henry Cornelius Agrippa (1486–1534) and Dr John Dee (1527–1608) used Hebrew and kabbalistic ideas in their magical experiments. Agrippa wrote *Three Books on Occult Philosophy*, which include lists of archangels for the planets, the days of the week, the mansions of the Moon and so on. Agrippa probably got much of his information about the angels from the Jewish mystical texts. Dr Dee was astrologer to Queen Elizabeth I; he consulted angels through a medium, and they gave him an angelic language called 'The Keys of Enoch'. Many of these magicians created incantations in Hebrew in order to call angels to do their bidding. Nowadays we want to co-create with angels, rather than summon them to carry out our orders.

The Renaissance philosophers' experiments with hidden mysteries initiated what is known as the Western Mystery Tradition. During the Age of the Enlightenment, which began in the late 17th century, ancient wisdom teachings and cosmological ideas fell out of favour, to be superseded by 'empirical science'. The new approach to science described itself as 'rational' (from *ratio*, meaning to measure) and scientists demanded measurable proof. But ancient wisdom does not die easily – it just goes underground.

The Occultists

In the late 19th century the esoteric or occult tradition started to flourish anew. One famous secret society, the Order of the Golden Dawn, used kabbalistic-style rituals based on occult philosophy. Founded in 1887, its members were middle-class spiritual seekers, including the poet W.B. Yeats (1865–1939). When they performed magical ceremonies the occultists used Hebrew invocations to summon the four archangels of the directions to banish negativity and strengthen the human system. One Golden Dawn member, Israel Regardie,[10] described the archangels as 'primordial archetypes: . . . nodal points which act as . . . power stations . . . through which the life stream flows and is . . . transmuted so as to be available to lower forms of life'.[11]

An offshoot of the Golden Dawn was a group called Alpha et Omega, founded in Paris in 1906. A well-known member was Dion Fortune (1890–1946), who reported having visions of Atlantis from the age of four and developed her psychic gifts before she was twenty. In her famous book *The Mystical Qabalah*[12] Dion Fortune identifies which archangels can be associated with each *sefira* on the Tree of Life, according to occult lore.

During this long period of occult development, from the Renaissance to the early 20th century, Kabbalah lost favour with Jewish scholars, who had mostly sidelined their mystical traditions after the Enlightenment. After all, Jewish rabbis who studied Kabbalah had been met with great distrust by people who thought they were magicians. Once Jewish scholars were permitted to attend university and study outside their own tradition, their very special form of mysticism, based on ancient knowledge, was largely dropped.

In the late 19th century, collections of Jewish legends were being compiled, notably by Louis Ginzberg, a German rabbi who in 1895 published a five-volume book, *The Legends of the Jews*, translated into English in 1908. These stories were regarded in the same way as the European fairytales collected by the Brothers Grimm (1812–14) – as enjoyable reading, but with no real spiritual meaning. However, I include some of them in this book. Many of these intriguing tales are very ancient – possibly as old as other Bible stories – and clearly come from a longstanding spiritual tradition.

It was the Western occultists who kept alive the idea of working with archangels and introduced the idea of 'decrees' – commands that would put the archangels to work for them. In the 20th century the occult tradition was continued by Elizabeth Clare Prophet (b. 1939) who perceived archangels as masculine and developed the idea (now incorporated into New Age teaching) that they must have feminine 'twin flames'.[13] The goal of the occultist was to become an 'adept', someone who has power over the material world. In this book I hope to encourage you to work with the archangels to take charge of your own destiny and develop the divine qualities that are within each of us, rather than to seek magical power – although once you take responsibility for your life you will find things unfolding in a magical way.

Archangels today

The angels keep their ancient places –
Turn but a stone, and start a wing!
'Tis ye, 'tis your estranged faces,
That miss the many-splendoured thing.
FRANCES THOMPSON

Until quite recently humanity's contacts with angels and archangels were a gift: celestial beings would make unexpected visits to people who were often living saintly lives. Today, this has changed radically. We can all learn to contact angelic beings, and receive from them support and guidance to help us in our daily lives. This change has come about with other changes in our religious and spiritual beliefs.

People originally believed that God lived in the skies (the words for 'heaven' and 'sky' are the same in Hebrew), and that archangels and other celestial helpers lived in the stars and planets. For the ancients, not only were these immortal beings literally above us, but also we were generally thought to be inferior to them. The gods or the angels looked down on us and we had to appease them in order for our lives to run smoothly.

Over time, these views have slowly changed. In the Gospel of Thomas, Jesus tells us that 'the kingdom of heaven is within you and within all creation', and mystics through the ages have told us that we all have God within us. Gradually, as science has revealed more answers to the mysteries of the universe and failed to reveal clusters of heavenly choristers in white nightgowns, people have abandoned many traditional notions about both God and celestial beings.

Modern physics tells us that every atom of Creation is buzzing with immense energy. Perhaps we can say that 'God' is this energy, a constant creative activity that manifests the many layers of reality; perhaps 'God' is a verb, rather than a noun. If we look at Creation in this way we can think of all the celestial 'beings' as celestial 'doings', essential activities that hold Creation in place. Our own thought patterns are also part of this creative process. If God and heaven are truly within us, this suggests that the archangels too can be reached by looking within ourselves, through meditation and inner journeying.

In the 1960s, while science was probing into outer space, many people were taking an interest in inner space. Some experimented with mind-expanding drugs, while others explored Eastern forms of meditation. The writer Aldous Huxley, who had mystical experiences after taking hallucinogenic drugs, believed that our everyday self filters out the vast wealth of information that we could potentially receive from the universe, so that we can survive – if we were to have direct experience of all reality at once we would be overwhelmed.[14] We can, however, expand our consciousness in a gentle way, by bringing meditation into our lives on a regular basis so that our connection to heaven becomes gradual, rather than overwhelming.

This recent revolution in collective consciousness has allowed more people to open up to other realms and receive channelled messages from archangels and other spiritual helpers, as happened to me. As well as going deep into my being I, like others, have often had the experience during meditation that my mind is expanding beyond my body and my everyday sense of self. The states of both expansion and depth are 'heavenly' and allow me to maintain an ongoing sense of connection to all Creation not just in the present, but through time – I experience myself as a timeless being. At times I feel myself going deep into my being so that I can retrieve memories of previous lives and ancient history.

In this deep state I access angelic messages and guidance. (Nowadays I am also often aware of angelic presences during my ordinary daily activities.) Meditation also allows me to have conversations with the archangels. Anyone can do this, if they are dedicated and prepared to commit their time – it is much more interesting than watching television! I tell all my students that meditation is essential 'technology' for anyone who wants to work with archangels.

A Meeting with Raphael

Archangels still make unexpected visits, of course – as my experience with Sandalphon shows. But they tend to arrive when the mind is not in an everyday waking state. They often come during dreams or daydreams, or in the stage between sleep and waking, when the mind is not distracted by external events. This is one man's account, from the archives of the Alister Hardy Religious Experience Research Centre (RERC).[15]

I awoke quite suddenly in the early hours and in the half-light I saw a cloaked and hooded figure standing by my bed. There was no illumination surrounding the figure and it appeared to be an ordinary person apart from the cloak and hood.

Then I had the feeling that my whole being was being drawn in a great sense of Love out towards this figure, and when this Being raised an arm over my upper body (I do not know whether it was part of the cloak that overshadowed me, or, believe it or not, a wing) I had the sensation of being part of a rushing, wind-like sound. Then my consciousness, or my spiritual self, left my physical body and I felt myself rising into a light, warmth, an overwhelming sense of Ultimate Being that increased as I rose upwards towards the cloaked arm or wing. It would be impossible to describe the nature or the brilliance of that Light as it increased in what must only have been milliseconds. Just when my spiritual being was on the point of no return to the physical level of consciousness I experienced the sensation of rising up against the 'wing' of the Being's arm, almost with a bump, and I returned almost unwillingly, as if pulled by a powerful elastic, back into that body on the bed.

Afterwards the name Raphael kept flooding my mind with great persistency and when I used a dowsing pendulum to ask if

> it had been Archangel Raphael who had given me that illuminating
> and life changing experience the answer was a very emphatic yes.
> The experience made me realise the insignificance of the physical
> vehicle of consciousness compared with the spiritual self.[16]

Modern perceptions of Archangels

Another important change in our experience of archangels today is
how we perceive them. Archangels in themselves have no gender:
they are beings of light and energy that take on a human aspect when
necessary. In the Bible and traditional stories and legends, they are
always described as masculine, and often given warrior-like characteristics. Michael, in particular, seems to be always involved in a battle[17]
and many famous paintings depict him wearing armour. Biblical and
medieval societies were patriarchal; women were meant to be passive
and were not expected to exercise power or choice over their own
destinies – though of course there were remarkable exceptions.

Nowadays we recognise that qualities that were traditionally
assigned to the two genders are not so easily defined, and we can
approach our dealings with the archangels with equal flexibility.
For example, I experienced the stern Archangel Samael, who teaches
self-discipline, as a woman with a white crystalline energy around
her (see p. 121). Some people experience Gabriel as feminine,
although I find 'him' boyish. Raphael, whose quality is soothing
and healing, also seems 'feminine', though men are quite capable
of working with this energy. And we can think of Michael as having
qualities of leadership and courage that do not always entail fighting.

The archangels all carry universal and timeless attributes, but how
we experience them is affected by the times we live in. These days
we don't necessarily see them with the traditional long robes and
wings – but they still appear, still bearing important spiritual messages.

A communication from Michael

The following story is told by the American writer Rosemary Ellen
Guiley in her first book about angels, *Angels of Mercy*.

Juliet Hollister, a deeply spiritual woman, was the founder of the Temple of Understanding, a large interfaith organisation. In October 1984, she was preparing for the sixth Spirit Summit Conference sponsored by the Temple, at the cathedral of St John the Divine in Manhattan. Up to 10,000 people were expected including the Dalai Lama and other religious leaders. Juliet was to deliver a fifteen-minute talk at the end, and she was very nervous beforehand.

Getting up after resting before the final rehearsal, Juliet suddenly became aware of a presence, a huge column of light standing at the foot of her bed. She perceived the outline of a figure and sensed it was an angel, though she did not see wings or a face. Juliet had already had encounters with angels, and though startled was not frightened. As she watched, the presence began to communicate with her telepathically.

'You're going to be speaking at the cathedral, and angels have a lot to do with holy, sacred places,' it told her. ' . . . On behalf of the angelic kingdom, we would appreciate it if, when you make your speech, you would tell the people that we are real, that we love the human race, and would like to work on its behalf. But we can't unless we're invited to do so. We don't enter the life of a human unless we're asked. We are very eager to help.'

Juliet was overwhelmed: never had she thought of saying anything about angels in her speech. She sensed that this was the Archangel Michael, and told him she would do anything to help the planet. But, not quite trusting herself, she continued: 'I'll do it if you do something to confirm I'm not hallucinating.'

She received the confirmation she needed [the story is told in the section on Archangel Michael, see p. 103] and at the conclusion of the conference – still fearing a sceptical response – Juliet told the audience that angels are real, and desire to help humanity, but they cannot do so unless humans ask for their help.

For weeks afterward, Juliet received an avalanche of mail about people's own beliefs and experiences with angels. 'They are real!' was the overall enthusiastic response.

Archangels and human possibilities

Each one of us is a fragment, a spark of the divine whole. We all have access to the variety of qualities carried by the different archangels and we can bring these into our everyday lives. We can think of notable human figures that manifest some of these qualities. Nelson Mandela, for example, is an ideal model of leadership who has lived with great courage in the face of adversity, standing by his principles throughout a long imprisonment. He manifests those spiritual qualities that the Archangel Michael encourages in us. Mother Teresa, who cared for the poor and sick in Calcutta, offering unconditional love wherever she saw pain and suffering, manifested the qualities represented by Zaphkiel, the Divine Mother.[18]

Divine energy has many attributes, and opposites are essential in the creative process. We have to be able to expand our vision and our creative possibilities, but not so far that we get lost in too many ideas, so we also need boundaries. So while one archangel will be encouraging and generous, another will be stern, bringing discipline into our lives. Often people prefer and need to work with a comforting healing angel like Raphael, but sometimes it's necessary to engage with an archangel like Hanael, who will help us become more assertive. As you work through this book you will learn how each archangel supports a different quality that you may need to develop.

How working with the Archangels can help you

And a new spirit I will put into you . . .
EZEKIEL 6.26

When you work with the archangels you are communicating with powerful cosmic forces that collaborate to shape the universe. The divine Creation is multi-dimensional and so is your soul, which is a miniature reflection of the whole Creation. So working with archangels allows you to take charge of your own mini-universe, of which you are the centre.

Meeting the Archangels of the Tree of Life, and then the Archangels of the Zodiac, will bring you into contact with different qualities that you can develop to enhance your life – such as courage (with help from Archangel Michael) and self-discipline (encouraged by Archangel Samael). The archangels will help you to understand why you are here, how to make appropriate choices and how to develop spiritual qualities that will enable you to function in the world more effectively.

The archangels can help you change unsatisfactory elements in your life. Perhaps you felt unloved as a child, and would welcome the motherly influence of Auriel. Perhaps you are unhappy with work, or you may be feeling a lack of abundance, or your relationships may be difficult. Each of the archangels is there to help you with a different aspect of living, such as Zadkiel, who will bring abundance into your life. Of course, the first step is your commitment to change, and you must be prepared to look at life in a new way – the archangels do not wave wands like fairy godmothers, but once you dedicate yourself to a new way of being they will support your spiritual progress.

How the Archangels helped Sarahjane

One of my students, Sarahjane, suffered from severe post-natal depression. She was unable to bond with her little girl Katie, and admitted that she was constantly screaming at her. Sarahjane was emotionally and physically exhausted. The pressure broke up her marriage and her husband walked out on her – things could not have got any worse.

> Katie was three when Sarahjane discovered the Invocation to the Archangels in my book *Living with Angels*. She knew she should try it out – she had nothing to lose. When Katie was asleep Sarahjane lit a white candle and imagined herself being cleansed by white light. Then she recited the invocation, calling on Gabriel, Raphael, Michael and Auriel in turn. Finally she asked to be filled with love and peace. 'I wanted to love my daughter like a mother should, so I shut my eyes and asked to be a better person.'
>
> Suddenly the room was bathed in golden light. 'It was like being asleep and someone switching on the lamp and when I opened my eyes I saw hundreds of twinkling lights. I shut my eyes again and reopened them to make sure I wasn't imagining things. The twinkling stars were still in my living room; then I watched them fade. Best of all, I felt calm and happy. That night I actually stood for an hour watching my daughter sleeping. My heart was bursting with love for her. That feeling didn't go away and we began to build a relationship.'

The Tree of Life and the Gates of Light

The Tree of Life is your map for a journey that will allow you, step by gentle step, to meet twelve powerful guides and mentors. They will help you uncover your strengths and weaknesses and rebalance your approach to life, and this in turn will produce wonderful changes in your everyday circumstances. You will gain the most benefit from working with them in order, starting with Sandalphon at the foot of the Tree, and working with them one at a time before moving on.

In Part 2 you will be meeting the twelve archangels associated with the *sefirot* (containers, or portals) of the Tree of Life, also called the Gates of Light. I have found them to be significant facilitators in the process of spiritual development. Diagram 1 on p. 38 shows you the names of the *sefirot*, which are all attributes of the Divine. These are useful to know because they help us to understand the qualities of the archangels. Diagram 2 on p. 39 shows you the archangels who relate to the *sefirot*: these are the Guardians of the Gates of Light. In Diagram 1 you will see that the left-hand 'pillar' of the Tree of Life is the 'passive', 'feminine' or 'yin' side, and the right-hand pillar is 'active', 'masculine' or 'yang'. The central pillar is the 'pillar of balance'. The Holy Spirit is neither masculine nor feminine, and its position is not regarded as a *sefira*. It marks the crossing point between the 'higher' and 'lower' *sefirot*, and this placement on the Tree gives us access to higher dimensions.

Before Creation starts unfolding everything is unified, but in order for the material world to come into being duality is necessary – dark and light, masculine and feminine, yin and yang. The pure energy of the Divine is only able to manifest all the beauty of Creation by dividing itself – just as a single egg divides when conception takes place. Once, when I was meditating during a Quaker meeting, I had a powerful image of divine white light, the pure energy of the universe. Then I saw that the light was an endless sheet of emptiness which had the potential to fold itself into anything and everything – the white sheet of light was like a huge piece of origami paper, continually folding, unfolding and refolding itself. There was no origami master involved in this process, no outside force, no 'creative designer': the sheet of light was itself both the paper and the artist.

I find this origami image useful – if you take a sheet of plain white paper, fold it once and stand it up like a tent, you will see that one side naturally falls into shadow. It is important in our modern work with archangels to realise that every one of the various divine qualities has its place, even those that seem challenging. 'Darkness' or 'shadows' are essential in the creative process and in our journey of self-development. The Tree of Life is holistic, and includes archangels we might regard as 'difficult' – later, for example, I will introduce you to Samael, who in some legends is described as a 'fallen' archangel and has been associated with Satan. If you cross-reference diagrams 1 and 2, you will see that Samael is in fact the archangel for the *sefira* Severity. Satan himself was originally an angelic being sent by God to test us, not the source of all evil.

The concept that there is an 'evil' force seeking to undermine human happiness only serves to disempower us. In Isaiah 45.7, God confirms that there is no outside source of evil: 'I am the Eternal God and there is no other. I form light and create darkness, I make peace and create evil.' The problems that have always faced humans have been created by humanity's bad behaviour – by our collective folly, ignorance, laziness and sometimes wickedness, not by the influence of a 'fallen angel'.

Although the Tree of Life comes from the kabbalistic tradition you do not have to know anything about Kabbalah in order to work with the archangels. When I set out all I had was the diagram, the names of the archangels – without knowing their Hebrew meanings – and the qualities of the *sefirot*. After I had my experience with Sandalphon I was determined to travel inwardly to meet the archangels, not just to read about them in a pile of dry old books. It was only in 2000 that I began my academic research and started to read some of those old books, so that I could compare my experiences with traditional material. I can therefore now share with you my own meetings with archangels, other modern archangel stories and information I have collected during my six years of research into angel stories in mystical and occult texts.

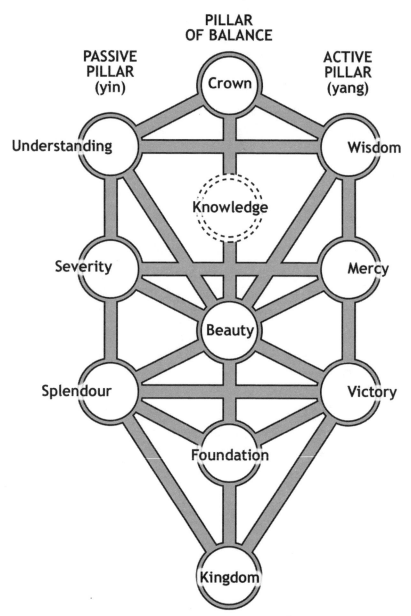

Diagram 1: The *sefirot* of the Tree of Life

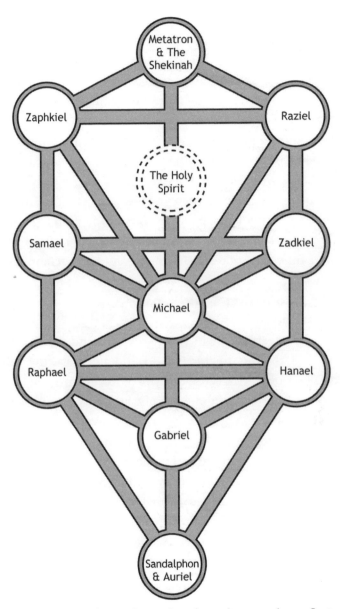

Diagram 2: The archangels who relate to the *sefirot*

Archangels who call to you

Each individual will find one of the twelve great archangels more appealing than the others. You will have natural characteristics that resonate more easily with their particular attributes: for example, you may be a natural healer and feel called by Raphael, or you may be a natural communicator and feel called by Gabriel. I have found that everyone has one archangel that will be significant in their life – I call this the Archangel of Destiny.

Sometimes an archangel may make you feel uncomfortable, or challenged in some way. This will indicate that you need to develop a quality that is weak in you. For example, if you feel uneasy with Samael's energy, it may be that you need to exercise more self-discipline, and accept the harsher lessons in life with a good grace. You will also find that some archangels will seem more significant at different times in your life. If you are studying, Gabriel will be a good ally. If you are recovering from a debilitating illness, Raphael will help you to recover, while Hanael will help you to get back on your feet and into action.

All the archangels can help you to awaken and direct your true potential, and to start to understand and integrate the different facets of your own character. As you become more whole and balanced, you can interact more fully and successfully with the outside world as well as the inner one, discovering new possibilities for yourself and breaking through old limitations. You will have a growing sense that you are in charge of your own life, and will feel able to take responsibility for what has happened already and design your future according to your true desires.

Before you can meet the archangels there is some important preparation you should do, so please read the next section, Getting Started, before setting off on the first part of your journey.

PART 2

The Journey – meeting the Twelve Archangels of the Tree of Life

Getting started

Now we come to the part of the book in which you can partici-
pate, if you want to, in meeting the Twelve Archangels of the Tree
of Life. You may simply prefer to read about these archangels, which
is fine, although for most people these pages offer a safe and fascin-
ating path of spiritual development, and the methods suggested
here are designed to be integrated into your everyday life. However,
since this is a deep journey offering the possibility of fundamental
transformation, it should be approached with respect.

This chapter outlines some useful aids for your journey, so please
read it with care. It is important to meet these archangels in their
order on the Tree of Life, starting from the foot of the Tree; this
will mean the process is grounded from the beginning.

Allocating your time

It will help to book yourself a regular slot for your archangel sessions,
perhaps once a fortnight. You will be dealing with powerful forces,
and will need time to integrate them. My SoulSchool students work
with no more than two archangels a month. Allow an afternoon
or evening, choosing a time when you will not be interrupted.
Setting a time in advance allows your unconscious mind to prepare
for meeting the next archangel, and if you know, for example, that
you have allocated yourself three hours on a particular evening,
you will be programming yourself to keep to that timeframe. This
will help you to create boundaries and you are much less likely to
have your everyday life interrupted by celestial messages!

I will be suggesting other things to do between sessions: these are practical activities that do not require meditation and will help to bring your inner understanding into your daily life.

Sharing with a friend

Whenever you are developing your spiritual wisdom, joining forces with a friend will enhance the experience beyond measure. You do not necessarily have to do the visualisations together – although that would be ideal. You could agree to do them on the same evening and call each other afterwards to compare notes. Even if you don't manage to synchronise your sessions it can be great to share notes with a fellow traveller.

Useful tools and preparation

Create a sacred space In the room you will be using, decorate a small table with coloured fabrics to create an 'altar', perhaps adding pictures or objects that seem suitable either generally or for the specific archangel you are working with. Include a candle to light before you start.

Prepare for a quiet time When you begin, make sure all phones are off. Keep any pets out of the room – cats especially are attracted to someone who is meditating, and can be a distraction. If you have small children, ask a partner or babysitter to take charge of them. And if you have teenagers, make sure they are out, or put a ban on loud music.

Incense and essential oils Use good-quality scented candles, essential oils or incense to scent the air. I suggest essential oils for use with each archangel, or you may prefer to choose a scent that feels good for you.

Crystals Each of the Archangels of the Tree of Life can be associated with a particular gemstone that was used in the breastplate of the High Priest in the ancient Jewish Temple. I include my suggestions at the top of each chapter in Part 2.

Bach Flower Remedies These can help you to integrate your spiritual and psychological process. Again, my suggestions are included at the top of each chapter in Part 2. Each remedy has been chosen to harmonise the energy of the archangel concerned.

Music Find music that suits you and helps you to relax, to play at the start of your session. You will find some suggestions about music in Appendix 2, p. 230.

Tibetan bells and singing bowls These create beautiful sounds whose vibrations clear the atmosphere. They are quite easy to obtain at Mind, Body and Spirit festivals or in New Age shops.

A journal of your work Get yourself a beautiful book to use as a journal. You could cover an inexpensive notebook with special paper or pictures. It is preferable to use unlined paper so that you can include coloured drawings or collages to record any visual impressions or feelings as well as writing notes. Have coloured pencils, pens or pastels at hand during your sessions.

Regular meditation

In addition to your regular archangel sessions, daily meditation can bring amazing improvements to all aspects of your life. It enables all your bodily functions to rest at a deeper level than during sleep. You become calmer and things that other people find stressful will leave you undisturbed. Moreover, when you come to do the visualisations your connection to the angelic realms will be deeper and faster. Using a mantra makes it easy to meditate (instructions can be found in Appendix 1) or you could obtain my *Quick and Easy Meditation* CD, available through the website www.workingwitharchangels.com.

Grounding exercise

When going on the kind of inner journeys you are about to embark on, it is important to know how to ground yourself both before and afterwards in order to maintain a solid connection with the real world. The following exercise is very effective.

ROOTING YOURSELF TO MOTHER EARTH

Sit quietly on your chair with your feet on the ground. Imagine that tiny filaments of light are stretching downwards from the soles of your feet; they are travelling down through the floor and through the foundations of your house. Like delicate, shining roots of gold and silver light they extend through the ground beneath the house, down, down and down until they reach a great crystal that sits in the very centre of the Earth itself. The crystal acts as an anchor for your roots and you can allow them to stay grounded at the core of the Earth throughout your session with the archangel.

Protection

Also before starting your sessions, you can invoke heavenly protection by calling on the archangels who support the four worlds and your four bodies – your spiritual, mental, emotional and physical bodies – using the invocation below.

INVOCATION TO THE ARCHANGELS

This invocation will protect your space while you are doing your angel work.

* ❖ Tidy your room so that it is free of clutter. Make sure you will not be disturbed. Light a candle and some incense that you enjoy.
* ❖ Take off your shoes. Stand in the middle of your room. Close your eyes and allow yourself to relax into a comfortable posture. Release any tension in your neck and shoulders, and allow your arms to hand loosely at your sides.
* ❖ Imagine gold and silver threads stretching from the soles of your feet down into the centre of the Earth, where a majestic crystal holds the energy for you.
  Now say the words of the invocation out loud:
  Auriel and Sandalphon, be my friends. Be present behind me as I walk my life's path.
  Gabriel, be my guide. Be present on my right hand as I communicate my needs and desires in the world.

Raphael, be my gentle adviser. Be at my left hand when I am relating to friends, family and all the strangers I meet.

Michael, be my protector. Walk ahead of me as I move forward into the unknown.

❖ Stand quietly for a moment, feeling the presence of the angels around you.

❖ Now, thank the archangels and say:

I take responsibility for my life and ask the angels to support my highest possibility.

❖ Reach your hands up towards the ceiling of your room, then bring them down in an arc on each side of you until they point towards the floor.

❖ Now visualise those gold and silver threads again and gently stamp your feet, wriggle your body, shrug your shoulders and breathe deeply before you open your eyes.[19]

A SYMBOL FOR PROTECTION

You can also visualise the Heavenly Protection symbol that is used in Shefa Healing.[20] Look at the symbol for a couple of moments, then stand up and close your eyes, breathe deeply and feel centred in your own being. Visualise the symbol as a shining shape on a deep blue background, like a night sky. The dots are like stars, and

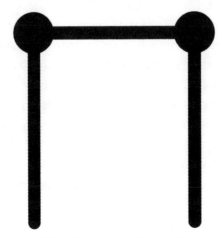

Diagram 3: The Heavenly Protection symbol

the lines are like white neon lights. Visualise the symbol expanding until the top bar is above your head and the two vertical lines are on each side of you. The symbol makes a protective 'tent' over you which is grounded as the two 'pillars' create boundaries for your energy, one on your right, one on your left.

You can then open your eyes and start your session, feeling the protection staying with you throughout.

You can use this symbol under all kinds of circumstances – when you are travelling, when you are giving healing or in any environment when you feel in need of protection.

Support from your Guardian Angel

There is a final piece of preparation to do before you embark on your journey, and that is to make contact with your Guardian Angel through the visualisation given below. If you have read my previous books you may already be familiar with this, and in touch with your Guardian Angel. If not, I recommend you to do it a week or so before beginning your journey with the archangels. Don't worry if you don't experience a strong visual image, or if very little seems to happen at first. Don't try too hard. You are opening connections that are new to you.

A JOURNEY TO MEET YOUR GUARDIAN ANGEL

The best way to use this visualisation is to make or obtain a recording of it. You can either read it on to a tape to play back to yourself, or download it as an MP3 file from www.workingwitharchangels.com.

Observe your breathing, allowing it to settle into a gentle rhythm. Breathe deeply, breathe slowly.

❖ Imagine you are in a very beautiful sitting room. You are sitting on a comfortable sofa, facing glass doors that open onto a wonderful garden. In your mind's eye you rise from the sofa and walk over to the doors. You open them carefully and step out into the garden.

❖ You wander through the garden where the colours of the flowers and the dewy grass seem brighter than anything you have ever seen. You can smell the perfume of the flowers and the newly mown grass. You can see butterflies flitting among the blossoms. You can hear birds singing in the clear blue sky above you.

❖ As you walk slowly through the garden you come to a gate, which leads out of the garden. You open the gate and find yourself in a country lane.

❖ You walk along the lane. On one side is a hedge full of birds and little animals. On the other is a field of corn with brightly coloured wild flowers – poppies, daisies and cornflowers.

❖ Eventually you come to some trees and find yourself wandering into a wood. The wood is quiet and you notice how the sun shimmers through the green and golden leaves.

❖ There is a path through the wood, marked with shining white stones. Although the trees are getting thicker, there seems to be a light ahead of you and you keep following the white stones until you come to a clearing, where the light comes from.

❖ In the clearing you find a shining building and you know that this is a sacred space which has been waiting for you.

❖ The door of your sacred building is open and you sense that a welcome awaits you. As you walk inside you know that you have come home. The door gently closes behind you, to provide a safe haven.

❖ You find yourself in a golden room with a seat waiting for you. When you sit down you feel peaceful, happy and content. This is the place where you will meet and talk to your Guardian Angel.

❖ Ask in your mind: 'I now call my Guardian Angel to come to me. I would like to know your name and please tell me anything I need to know which is important to me at this stage on my life path.'

❖ **Allow three minutes' silence at this point, so that you can talk to your Guardian Angel.**

❖ Now say thank you to your Guardian Angel and get up from your seat. Move gently towards the door of your sacred room.

❖ You can still feel the presence of your Guardian Angel. As the doors open gently you step outside and start moving down the path of white stones which guides you through the wood.

❖ Gradually the trees begin to thin out and you can see the sun shining through the leaves.

❖ You find yourself back on the path through the country. The hedge with birds and wild animals is on one side of you. The swaying golden corn and the wild flowers, scarlet poppies, white daisies and bright blue cornflowers are on the other.

❖ Eventually you find the gate that leads back into the garden, and you wander through the garden, smelling the flowers and listening to the birds singing and the bees humming.

❖ You walk towards the house and step back through the glass doors into the sitting room.

❖ Walk back to the comfortable sofa and sit down once more.

❖ Before opening your eyes, breathe deeply and stretch your body like a cat. Shrug your shoulders and wriggle your hands and feet.

❖ You may need to take some time before you open your eyes. When you do, remember to look down at the floor first. Coming back into everyday reality should be a gentle process, as outlined in the exercise below.

COMING OUT OF MEDITATION OR VISUALISATION SESSIONS

Before opening your eyes, put your attention on the different areas of your body, and use your hands to affirm to yourself that you exist in the physical body. Feel, squeeze or rub your limbs, rotate your shoulders, and wriggle your hands and feet. Stretch like a cat.

When you open your eyes, gaze downwards, so that the first thing you see is your own body and the floor beneath your feet. You may like to open and close your eyes a couple of times, allowing visual impressions of the outside world to come back gently into your consciousness. Drink a glass of water. If you want to draw a picture of your experience, or write down your Guardian Angel's message, do it now. If you did not receive a verbal message, don't worry about this. The answer may come to you later – in a dream, in someone's words, or in a book you happen to pick up.

Afterwards, stand up and move around some more. You may wish to have a small snack, which will help you to be grounded.

Meeting the Archangels

In the following chapters you will be meeting each of the twelve archangels through a guided visualisation, which you can record beforehand or download from www.workingwitharchangels.com. The visualisations are identical, apart from the words you will speak to the individual archangels and the invocation to each archangel included in each chapter.

Before starting each session, tape-record the visualisation, including the words addressed to the archangel you are working with. Make sure you will not be disturbed: switch off all phones and find yourself a quiet space. Make yourself a small altar, placing on it the items you have collected to represent the archangel's energy. Create a pleasant ambience by playing some music beforehand, or by sounding Tibetan bells or bowls, and by lighting incense. Then light your chosen candle, asking for divine protection as you set out on your spiritual journey.

Now either sit or lie down comfortably, and start listening to your tape.

VISUALISATION TO MEET THE ARCHANGELS – TO BE TAPE-RECORDED

❖ Begin by asking your Guardian Angel to accompany you on your journey.

❖ With your Guardian Angel beside you, you find yourself on a path, walking towards a beautiful building that gleams in the sunshine.

❖ There is a gate at the front of the building, made of golden filigree.

❖ As you watch, the gate gently swings open and you can see a light shining beyond the entrance.

❖ Your Guardian Angel is with you as you move through the gate and beneath an arch into the central hall of the building where beautiful music fills the atmosphere.

❖ The hall is vast, with high ceilings, and around the edges you can see many doors shining with different-coloured crystals. Each door has the name of an archangel engraved on it.

❖ Now ask to meet the archangel you have chosen.

❖ Your Guardian Angel gently guides you towards one of the shining doors.

❖ The door seems to dissolve in front of you and you become aware of a wonderful presence.

❖ **At this point record the words you will speak to the archangel you are meeting.**

❖ Now sit quietly for a few moments and be open to the archangel's response.

❖ **Leave at least three minutes unrecorded on your tape.**

❖ Now thank the archangel for being with you.

❖ Ask your Guardian Angel to take you back through the garden so that you can leave by the shining gate. Turn around to look at the beautiful building and watch as the gate gently swings back into place.

❖ **End of recording.**

❖ Now breathe deeply, stretch your limbs, open your eyes and gently come out of your meditation. Record your experiences in your journal. Before blowing out the candle, recite the invocation to the archangel you have met, and send the light to someone who may need angelic help.

Messages and gifts

As you can see, the above visualisation includes a space for the archangel to communicate with you and perhaps to give you a message or a gift. Don't worry if you don't receive this clearly during the visualisation. You may have a significant dream during the days following, or a message may come to you from a passage in a book or through another person. Look out for an unexpected gift in your everyday life. (Gifts are usually symbolic and meaningful to the person concerned – such as a crystal, a pen, a sword or a book.)

If you still feel you have experienced nothing, you can make the journey again at a later date. In order to work with the archangels we often have to shift old blocks in our psyche, and sometimes this takes a while.

Now you are ready to begin your journey, starting at the foot of the Tree and then moving up one step at a time until you reach the top.

Sandalphon: the Guardian

Also spelt: Sandolphon, Sandolfon

Have you read in the Talmud of old,
In the Legends the Rabbins have told
Of the limitless realms of the air –
Have you read it, the marvellous story
Of Sandalphon, the Angel of Glory,
Sandalphon the Angel of Prayer?
HENRY WADSWORTH LONGFELLOW

Sefira:	Kingdom
Keywords:	Trust, reliability, stewardship
Colours:	Terracotta, golden brown, stone
Gemstone:	Jasper
Flower remedy:	Gentian
Essential oil:	Frankincense
Planet:	Earth

About Sandalphon

No one knows why Sandalphon has a Greek name, unlike most of his colleagues, whose names are Hebrew. The only other archangel you are going to meet with a Greek name is Metatron, the archangel at the top of the Tree of Life, who is known as Sandalphon's twin brother. It is possible that his name means 'co-brother', though it's more likely that it means 'one who wears sandals' (from the Greek word *sandalon*). When I first met Sandalphon in my vision, he was wearing simple sandals. The *Zohar* tells us that he wears sandals or soft shoes when he is meeting the Creator, and leather shoes when he is in the presence of the Shekinah, the bride of Metatron.

Stories concerning Sandalphon

Only two archangels have lived as human beings – Sandalphon, who was the prophet Elijah and his twin brother Metatron, who lived as the prophet Enoch. Both Elijah and Sandalphon have been associated with the Messiah, the divine messenger whose task is to help humanity raise its level of spirituality and bring peace on Earth. The Bible tells us that Elijah brought a widow's only son back to life (I Kings 17.17–24). Jesus, visiting the city of Nain, also brought a widow's son back from the dead (Luke 7.11–15). Miracles like this prompted his followers to ask Jesus if he was Elijah returned. The story also goes that instead of dying, at the end of his life Elijah was swept in a fiery chariot up into heaven, where he was transformed into the Archangel Sandalphon.

Unlike some of the other prophets, who experienced God in the midst of dramatic, awe-inspiring visions, Elijah heard God as a 'still, small voice' (2 Kings 2.1–2). Sandalphon brings that same calmness with him when he asks us to put our trust in the Divine. The lamb that appeared with him in my vision reminds us that Sandalphon's energy is gentle, sweet and quite playful – masculine, but brotherly, rather than fatherly. He was also carrying an olive branch, an ancient symbol for peace.

A Kabbalist meets Sandalphon

The story of Rabbi Joseph della Reina (1418–72) illustrates how a Renaissance mystic would prepare very carefully to meet the archangels. Joseph was a kabbalist living in Spain at a time when Jews were being persecuted by the Spanish Catholics. Wanting to rid the world of evil, Joseph gathered his disciples in order to ask for angelic help. First, Elijah appeared to them and on his instructions they purified themselves, fasting and praying for 21 days, and smelling incense, to prepare to meet the Archangel Sandalphon.

When the archangel appeared, they were to wrap themselves in prayer shawls and cover their faces.

Sandalphon arrived in a fiery chariot with a great host of angels. He told Joseph sternly that sons of Adam should have very good reasons before calling celestial beings down to Earth. Joseph was trembling but, fortified by his frankincense, he found the words to explain his mission. Sandalphon put a reassuring hand on Joseph, but warned him that ridding the world of evil was not a task that humans could achieve without help: even Sandalphon was not powerful enough to conquer evil alone and other archangels would have to be involved.[21]

The tall Archangel

Sandalphon is also unimaginably tall, the tallest of all the angels. According to Jewish legend, when the patriarch Moses was taken to the Third Heaven, he caught sight of Sandalphon and called him 'the tall angel'. In my own vision his brilliant, radiant halo seemed to disappear into the sky. How far can a person walk in 500 years? It is said that that is how much taller Sandalphon is than the great Metatron himself. While his sandalled feet are always in touch with the Earth, as our trustworthy guide he is tall enough to contact the more subtle dimensions of heaven.

One of Sandalphon's most important tasks is to carry the prayers of human beings up to heaven, and in order to do this he weaves them into garlands. He is also described as a *hazzan*, a master of song, and I have always imagined these garlands as threads of sound and colour made up of the vibrations of our heartfelt desires and wishes. Sandalphon uses his mastery of sound to gather our prayers into a powerful message that is directed straight to the divine source.

As the first archangel on the Tree of Life Sandalphon is close to its roots, and to the Earth. This is a good place for you to begin your own journey – with Sandalphon you will start by being well grounded. Beside him stands his female companion, Auriel, the next archangel you will be meeting.

Sandalphon is the Archangel for planet Earth. He represents the presence of the Almighty in every molecule of the created world, so we can find him in gardens, in the wilderness, in rocks, stones, trees and every grain of sand on the seashore. He is an environmental archangel and he asks us to respect planet Earth, so that it will flourish and become a heavenly place for us all to live in for many generations to come.

Visions of Sandalphon today

You will have read the description of my vision of Sandalphon in the Introduction. My friend Kathleen Pepper, who also works with angels, sent the following story to me.

PRAYERS FOR THE PRINCESS

For many years I have been aware of angels and have been able to visualise them and tune in to their presence. In 1997 the world was stunned to hear of Princess Diana's sudden death, and thousands of bouquets were left outside Buckingham Palace and Kensington Palace where she lived.

After the funeral, I felt inspired to go to London to look at the flowers, and my husband came with me. As we walked among the crowds towards Kensington Palace the perfume of roses and lilies was overpowering, coming from the millions of flowers laid outside the palace gates. A friend who was a flight attendant at the time said that from the air they made the shape of a heart.

We stood there for quite a while and I began to meditate about the event. As I meditated, I became aware of an enormous angel standing in the centre of an area that was cordoned off. It was so enormous that it seemed to reach right up to the sky.

I saw the angel gathering the feelings of devotion and grief and using them for the benefit of the country, in fact for the world. These feelings appeared as an enormous radiation of light from the heart centre of the angel. The emotion I felt was so powerful that there were tears in my eyes.

Early in 1998, a friend of mine told me about Theolyn's *Angel Script* cards, as I was facilitating angel workshops. When I read the description of Sandalphon, I knew that he was the angel I had seen, because of his great height.

During the next few years I had several telephone conversations with Theolyn, and it was she who told me that Sandalphon weaves prayers into garlands, which I hadn't known before. I think the angels give clues to different people as if we are putting a jigsaw puzzle together. Each of us gets a piece and, as they fit together, the picture grows bigger and more complete.

Sandalphon also has a reputation for helping in emergencies. Sandalphon rescued Maureen, a lecturer at the University of Wales, after she lost a bag of valuables, including her passport.

SANDALPHON THE HELPER

In the summer of 1995, during a coach journey to visit a friend in Wakefield, Maureen's handbag was stolen, and she missed her connection. By the time she arrived she was quite distressed. Her friend took her shopping to replace the things she needed immediately, but as it was after office hours they decided to wait until next day to deal with Maureen's missing documents, including her passport, visa and tickets. Maureen's friend assured her that she had no need to worry – it would all be sorted out. Then she asked her if she believed in angels. Maureen said she did, though she wasn't exactly sure what they were.

Her friend took her to Wakefield Cathedral, where there is an angel altar, to appeal for the return of her bag. At the altar Maureen said a prayer and sat down to meditate and restore her equilibrium. Minutes later she was suddenly shocked out of her meditation by the appearance of two enormous eyes close to her face – she was too shaken to continue meditating. Her friend thought this might be the appearance of an angel, but wasn't sure which one.

Three days later the Newcastle police telephoned: they had recovered Maureen's bag. When she collected it she was surprised to find the contents almost intact, including some money she'd hidden in a secret pocket.

Back in London, hoping to learn more about the angel she'd seen, Maureen decided to go to a workshop given by Julie Soskin at the College of Psychic Studies. Scanning a list of angels to see which 'resonated' with her, she kept returning to two names, Metatron and Sandalphon, neither of whom she'd heard of, and Julie told her that they were twins. The following year Maureen had an Aura Soma reading. The first thing she was told was that Sandalphon was taking care of her and her earthly needs.

Maureen's story demonstrates how we can often receive help without knowing at the time who the helper is.

Calling on Sandalphon

When would you want to call on this powerful archangel? Before doing the visualisation, ask yourself these questions:

❖ Do I have confidence that Creation will support me?
❖ Do I believe that I can manifest what I need in my life?
❖ Am I certain that my life purpose will unfold according to plan?

Sandalphon encourages trust and a sense of material security. He walks the Earth but his head reaches heaven; in the same way human beings have the potential to lead lives that are both spiritual and material. In order to create a life that you love, you need to feel supported by Creation.

Preparing for your journey to meet Archangel Sandalphon

For a few days before going on this journey, start gathering together items to place on your altar that will remind you of Sandalphon's energy: terracotta or stone-coloured scarves, a gemstone, other special stones or pebbles, pictures of landscapes, feathers. Have fun and be open to discovery rather than having a set idea about what you need. Find a suitably coloured or scented candle.

Pre-record the visualisation given on pages 52–3, or download it from www.workingwitharchangels.com, and follow the instructions for beginning your session. Here are the words to speak to Sandalphon (to be included in your recording):

Sandalphon, guardian and brother to all humanity, please let me feel your presence in my life so that I can experience the true joy of being in a trusting relationship with the Divine.

Help me to manifest what I need in my life and to grow in confidence as my life purpose unfolds according to plan.

Please tell me if there are any changes I can make in my life to create more harmony and peace in the world, for myself, for all the people I love, and for my brothers and sisters around the world.

If you have a gift for me to help me on my way, I am willing to receive it into my life.

Come out of your meditation as described on pages 50–1, and then recite the following invocation. Send the light to anyone who may need angelic help before blowing out your candle.

INVOCATION TO SANDALPHON

Sandalphon, archangel and guardian of this planet I live on, help me to trust in the natural processes of creation and to be well grounded and responsible in the work I do here. In my daily life I wish to balance the spiritual with the material. I seek only to create harmony and I ask you to support me in my efforts.

Other ways to bring Sandalphon into your life

❖ Create an icon. Copy the invocation to Sandalphon on an A4 piece of card (or you could photocopy it from the book and stick it on to the card). Around the invocation, create a collage of pictures that remind you of Sandalphon's energy. You can glue on pieces of coloured fabric, feathers and cut-outs from magazines. Put your finished icon where you can see it while you are working with Sandalphon.

❖ Commit yourself to a task that will improve your local environment. Check that you are doing all you can to conserve energy and recycle everyday consumables, such as paper, plastic and glass.

❖ Dedicate your daily meditation to sending peace to trouble spots in the world.

❖ Make contact with anyone who is organising a campaign for improving the local environment – such as clearing brambles from footpaths, or raising funds to refurbish your community hall.

❖ Find a grassy place where you can walk barefoot, feeling the ground beneath you. Stretch out your arms towards the sky and drink in the sensation of being grounded on Earth while connected to the whole cosmos. It's wonderful to do this at night, under a starry sky.

❖ Plant something and nurture it daily – even if you only have a window box.

❖ Get away from your usual environment to a place where you can commune with nature and feel the energy of the Divine – even a city park will have a corner where you can feel this connection.

Whenever you are in doubt, or find your mind filling with anxieties about the future, allow yourself to relax into the arms of Sandalphon. If you put your trust in him, he can help to bring your visions into reality – but if you fret and worry, negative energy may block the perfect outcome. Do what you can, then leave Sandalphon to weave your wishes into a heavenly garland. The loving power of the Divine will do the rest.

Auriel: the Companion

Also spelt: Uriel, Oriel

The blessed damozel lean'd out
From the gold bar of Heaven;
Her eyes were deeper than the depth
Of waters still'd at even;
She had three lilies in her hand,
And the stars on her hair were seven.
DANTE GABRIEL ROSSETTI

Sefira:	Kingdom
Keywords:	Salvation, tender loving care, mending hurts, grace
Colours:	Silver and pale blue
Gemstone:	Beryl
Flower remedy:	Chicory
Essential oil:	Jasmine
Planet:	The Moon

About Auriel

Auriel's name means 'Light of God'; it is often spelt Uriel. Archangels' names can vary in spelling because biblical Hebrew writing has no vowels.

I associate the Moon with the Archangel Auriel. The Moon is the 'consort' of our planet Earth because she does not simply circle the Earth but dances with our planet around a common centre. The Earth and the Moon form what astronomers call a 'binary system' – two heavenly bodies bound together as they move around the skies. Similarly Auriel is like a bride to Sandalphon, who is the steward of planet Earth. In traditional Kabbalah and in the work of Rudolf Steiner, Gabriel is associated with the Moon but, as I explain later, I believe Gabriel has a stronger connection with Mercury.

In many accounts Auriel is referred to as a 'prince' or 'regent'. Like God and all the other archangels, Auriel was traditionally regarded as male in the past, but many of the qualities associated with this archangel can be seen as feminine. In traditional Kabbalah Auriel does not appear as an archangel on the Tree of Life, but you will understand from the account of my vision of Auriel below why I feel secure in including 'her' as the consort of Sandalphon.

Stories concerning Auriel

Auriel appears in a number of ancient stories, many of them added to over time in Hebrew commentaries and myths. For instance, although an archangel, Auriel has been named as one of the cherubim who stood at the gate of Eden with a fiery sword when Adam and Eve were expelled from Paradise (the Book of Adam and Eve).[22] Auriel has also been described as a seraph.

An early reference is in the Book of Enoch,[23] where Auriel is mentioned as one of the 'four angels of the Presence' who surround the throne of God and govern the four directions (Enoch 9.1). Enoch also describes Auriel as the governor of all angels, and tells the reader that God set Auriel to rule over all the stars and the planets in the skies. In this story Auriel guides the prophet Enoch to the upper heavens. Here Auriel joins with Michael, Gabriel and Raphael to voice their concerns about humanity, which has become progressively more warlike. The archangels ask God to bring an end to the bloodshed and violence, so God sends Auriel to Noah to warn him about the impending flood which will 'end all flesh' except for Noah, his family and the creatures that he rescues in his ark.

In the Book of Esdras,[24] Auriel appears to another prophet called Ezra, and answers his questions about the state of the world and the divine plan for the Israelites, as well as for the people of the whole world. According to the *Zohar*, Auriel provided supernatural lights to guide the children of Israel when they left Egypt (Exodus 19.1). During the Exodus which followed, when the Israelites spent 40 years wandering in the desert, Auriel was in charge of 365 groups of angels – the same number as the days of the year – each with a key to the hidden lights that hold the secrets to the universe.

According to one story, when God commanded Abraham to leave home and become the father of a new nation, it was Auriel who led Abraham out of the city of Ur. Another legend tells us that it was Auriel who gave the Kabbalah to humanity. Auriel is sometimes included with Gabriel and Michael in stories about the burial of Moses.

The *Zohar* informs us that Auriel had a special function in the Jewish Temple. When a sacrifice was made, Auriel would appear on the altar in the likeness of a lion and receive the offering on God's behalf. The altar was called Ariel – *ari* is Hebrew for 'lion' – and when the archangel arrived the priests and the Israelites all rejoiced, because they knew that their sacrifices had been accepted with favour. The appearance of Auriel in the altar fire encouraged everyone present to have a change of heart, and to repent of their old attitudes and behaviour. This is why Auriel has become known as an angel of salvation, or grace.

Jacob and the Angel

The Hebrew patriarch Jacob (whose son Joseph was sold into slavery by his jealous brothers) had several encounters with angels, including his famous dream of a ladder ascending to all the way to heaven, with angels going up and down it (Genesis 28.12–22). Later (in a story often painted by artists) the Bible tells us how Jacob, about to be reconciled with his brother, wrestled all night with a 'man' and although badly injured in the thigh would not give up until his opponent gave him his blessing. Eventually, by morning, the 'man' gave Jacob a blessing and a new name – Israel, which means 'he who wrestles with God' (Genesis 32.24–29). This unnamed 'man' has always been regarded as an angel, and Jewish mystical tradition has it that this was Auriel.

Visions of Auriel today

Although you will find Auriel at the foot of the Tree of Life with Sandalphon, she was the very last archangel I asked to meet. When I first discovered the Tree of Life I worked with the traditional archangels and it wasn't until I had completed my journey up the Tree, meeting only eleven archangels, that I realised that two significant elements were missing. First, the Archangel Uriel (I only knew this spelling at the time) was absent: the other three from the well-known set of four were on the Tree, but not 'Uriel'. Second, I wondered why Metatron should have a feminine companion, the Shekinah, but not Sandalphon, who is Metatron's twin.

Then I came across the story of how the Shekinah withdrew her presence from the Earth after Adam and Eve were expelled from Paradise, and would only return when humans learned how to behave properly. I had a sudden revelation. Perhaps the place of Uriel, who is associated with the element of earth, was beside Sandalphon at the foot of the Tree, as his consort. Maybe Uriel, as angel of grace, was a feminine principle who could help to counteract the over-emphasis on the masculine that has been so harmful for humanity and the planet. I decided to use the spelling Auriel, to make a point that we should think about 'her' in this way.

MY VISION OF AURIEL

When I asked to meet Auriel as Sandalphon's bride, I saw her as a mother figure with a child, like the Egyptian goddess Isis with Horus, or Mary with Jesus. She stood on the seashore, holding a lily, surrounded by long grasses and bright flowers. Quietly sitting at Auriel's feet was a majestic lion. The water made a gentle 'sssh' sound and gradually the sky darkened and stars and a crescent Moon appeared behind her. Auriel was tall, like Sandalphon, and the stars seemed to make a crown for her head. A few nights later

I had a dream in which both Auriel and Sandalphon appeared holding hands. They were standing on a hill surrounded by a country landscape busy with small animals and birds. The sun shone down on them and they seemed slightly transparent. Gradually they faded, and I woke up with a sense of well-being and wholeness.

Since having this vision, I have introduced Auriel to all my students as a feminine archangel, companion to Sandalphon at the foot of the Tree of Life, so that we can collectively encourage male and female energies to work harmoniously together. Auriel's lion made me think of the strength card in the Tarot pack, which represents a woman who is strong in self-knowledge – it was not until much later that I read that this archangel would descend to the altar in the shape of a lion. I had already seen Sandalphon with a lamb beside him, representing the development of gentle qualities in men, and it made me think of the prophecy that there would be a peaceable kingdom on Earth, when 'the lion will lie down with the lamb'.

Auriel with her small child had reminded me of Mary, the mother of Jesus, who is often called Queen of the Angels. One of my students, Ellen, met Auriel as a queen when she began her Tree of Life journey. Here is her account.

THE QUEEN OF THE KINGDOM

I imagined myself sitting down in a leafy glade with my back against a tree. I could see nature spirits making daisy chains and they placed them round my neck and on my head. They guided me to a stream where a boat was waiting for me. I travelled in the boat until we arrived at a place where a large oak tree grew, its old roots creating an underground tunnel. The spirits guided me down into the tunnel, which was dark at first – although I didn't feel afraid.

Then we came into a room that seemed to be made of crystal, it was shining so brightly, and I saw the queen of the kingdom sitting on a golden throne. She was dressed in velvet and wore a golden crown. She leaned towards me, opened her hand and offered me a precious stone. The queen told me how differently things work in her realm of light. In her world everyone works together harmoniously, but humans work for themselves, holding on tightly to everything they own. We need to let go, trusting that there is plenty of love, plenty of food and other material things. If we share what we have everyone will benefit and this generosity will come back to us.

Calling on Auriel

Our success in the world and our ability to follow through our life choices depends on our having a sense of self-worth. Auriel nurtures our inner child and encourages emotional security. She reassures us and supports us, so that we feel comfortable in everything we do. Before meeting her, think about the following questions:

❖ Do you feel loved?
❖ Do you feel anxious about expressing your true self?
❖ Do you feel able to deal with negative emotional issues?

Auriel can help you move forward into a new way of being. She will reassure you of your value as a person and will be a gentle guiding hand as you travel on your life path.

Your journey to meet Archangel Auriel

Now you can prepare to meet Auriel. Make an appointment in your mental diary and begin collecting the accessories that will help you tune in to Auriel's energy: pictures of the Moon, images you associate with strong mother qualities, silver and pale blue fabrics, crystals, flowers – perhaps you could find a lily. Candles or incense scented with jasmine will help to create a gentle mood.

Pre-record the visualisation on pages 52–3, or download it from www.workingwitharchangels.com, and follow the instructions for beginning your session. Here are the words to speak to Auriel (to be included in your recording):

Auriel, gentle companion to all humanity, please let me feel your presence in my life so that I can experience the tender loving care of the Divine.

Help me to become more aware of the constant presence of the divine love that nurtures and sustains us in Creation, so that I can let go of any anxiety and self-doubt.

Please help me avoid judging people and events, so that I can approach life with an open heart and appreciate divinity in every moment and in everyone I meet.

If you have a gift for me to help me on my way, I am willing to receive it into my life.

Come out of your meditation as described on pages 50–1, and speak the following invocation. Remember to send the light to anyone who may need angelic help before blowing out your candle.

INVOCATION TO ARCHANGEL AURIEL

Auriel, archangel and companion, light of God, watch over me and nurture me. I am trying to walk a path that is gentle and harmless, please provide me with a guiding light. Reassure me when I feel lost and uncertain. Help me open my heart so that I can give love generously.

Other ways to bring Auriel into your life

❖ Create your own image to represent your experience of Auriel; if you received a message you would like to keep, you could include this. Or copy the invocation to Auriel on an A4 piece of card, decorating it with colours or a collage of pictures and fabrics. Put your finished icon where you can see it while you are working with Auriel.

❖ Do something that will make someone else feel nurtured and loved. You could help a busy friend with household chores while they luxuriate in a long bath – take round a candle and some sweet-smelling bath salts. In this way you will bring the energy of Auriel into their life.

❖ Find a practical way of helping someone who may be feeling unloved. Perhaps you could write to a prisoner, or collect a fund to provide birthday or Christmas gifts for children in a local home.

❖ When you are out and about, make a point of smiling or saying something friendly to people, especially the ones who seem grumpy, depressed or angry.

❖ Watch the phases of the Moon as she changes through the month; this will remind you that even when there is darkness the light always returns.

❖ Visit a natural beauty spot where you can be close to water. Sit quietly there. If you can go at dusk when the stars are coming out you will feel a sense of belonging to Creation.

On any occasion when you feel lonely, or lost, close your eyes and acknowledge that Auriel, the Divine Companion, is a constant friend and generous mother who gives us all unconditional love. When you open your heart to this love you will be filled with a sense of comfort and love will overflow into your everyday life. If you give your tender loving care freely to others, this will come back to you a thousand-fold and your life will be filled with blessings.

Gabriel: the Messenger

Also spelt: Gavriel; Islamic
spellings: Jibrael, Jibril

Heaven's Golden-winged Herald, late hee saw
To a poor Galilean virgin sent.
How low the Bright Youth bow'd
and with what awe
Immortall flowers to her faire hand present.
RICHARD CRASHAW

Sefira:	Foundation
Keywords:	Change, messages, spiritual growth, signs, guidance
Colours:	Green, turquoise
Gemstone:	Emerald
Flower remedy:	Scleranthus
Essential oil:	Cedarwood
Planet:	Mercury

About Gabriel

Gabriel's name is usually translated as 'God is my strength'; the Hebrew word *gaver* literally means 'a man', but implies strength and power. In occult tradition[25] and in the work of the Austrian visionary Rudolf Steiner, Gabriel is associated with the Moon. But he has some similarities with Mercury: his tasks are mostly to do with communication, which in astrology is a function of Mercury. Gabriel often assists at the deaths of holy people, and Mercury is also described as a *psychopompos* – someone who helps the living pass over into death.

Stories concerning Gabriel

Gabriel is probably the most famous and the most written about of all the archangels. His appearances are linked with two significant chapters in the story of religion: he announced the coming of Jesus to Mary (Luke 1.26) and, in Muslim tradition, he dictated the Holy Koran, verse by verse, to the Prophet Mahomet. Before visiting the Virgin Mary, Gabriel also appeared in the Temple to announce that Elizabeth, Mary's aged and childless kinswoman, would give birth to a son, John – later known as John the Baptist (Luke 1.11–18). In this account Gabriel appears on the right side of the altar; elsewhere it is said that he stands on the right-hand side of God's throne, with Michael on the left.

Apart from Michael, Gabriel is the only archangel[26] mentioned by name in both the Hebrew Bible and the Christian gospels. The earliest biblical account of Gabriel is in the Book of Daniel. The prophet Daniel was exiled in Babylon (586–38 BC), where he and his fellow Jews were subject to the harsh rule of kings who followed their own gods. Daniel tells us that during the reign of King Belshazzar he received a vision of a ram and a goat fighting, which apparently foretold great danger. Standing by the banks of a river, trying to understand the vision, Daniel saw someone who looked like a man and a human voice called out: 'Gabriel, make this man understand the vision.' As Gabriel approached, Daniel fell to the ground in fear, but the archangel pulled him to his feet and explained the meaning of the vision (Daniel 8.16–27).

Later, Daniel was in mourning for three weeks, eating no 'meat or wine'. After this fast he had another vision by the river:

I saw a man clothed in linen with a belt of gold from Ophir round his waist. His body gleamed like topaz, his face shone like lightning, his eyes flamed like torches, his arms and legs sparkled like a disc of bronze, and when he spoke his voice sounded like the voice of a multitude. (Daniel 10.4–7)

Once more Daniel fell down and was again raised up by the magnificent being that called him 'a man greatly beloved'. Gabriel's name is not mentioned here, but most scholars believe that Daniel was referring to the same archangel as before. Daniel described his visitor as 'a man clothed in linen', and the *Zohar* explains that since Gabriel was appointed to be a messenger he had to be clothed in the garments of this world.[27]

Gabriel also appears in Jewish mystical stories as the heavenly author of mysterious writing. In another story from Daniel, King Belshazzar was holding a feast when a message appeared on the palace wall, written by a disembodied hand (Daniel 5.5). Daniel, who had already interpreted dreams for the king, was summoned to unravel its meaning. He told the king something he did not want to hear: that his days were numbered, and that he had been weighed in the balance and found wanting and his kingdom would be given to his enemies. That very night the king died and his kingdom was taken over by Darius the Mede. This story led rabbis to wonder whether the hand belonged to an angel and Gabriel was an obvious contender.

Later mystics believed that God could communicate through automatic writing, or by speaking through a prophet – what we nowadays call 'channelling'. The communicating angel was called a *maggid*, a sayer, and there are many stories about divine revelations received in this way by mystics who were prepared to fast for several days. The Jewish kabbalists concluded that the writing was done by Gabriel, although Michael was also involved – he is called 'the scribe'. Usually a scribe does the actual writing, but perhaps in this joint arrangement Michael provided the dictation.

Gabriel and Michael often appear together in traditional stories. In one delightful tale[28] King Solomon, warned by a prophecy that his daughter would marry a poor man, locked her up in a high tower. A travelling scholar, seeking somewhere to sleep, found the skin of an ox near the tower and curled up in it for the night. A hungry vulture lifted up the remains of the ox and carried it, with the scholar inside, to the top of the tower. When the princess saw this handsome young man she asked him to marry her, and since there were no humans present, the betrothal was witnessed by the two archangels Gabriel and Michael. King Solomon was delighted because, although he had tried to evade the prophecy, the young man was not only handsome but also learned – and the king himself was a great seeker after wisdom. Such are the ways of the Divine!

Gabriel is often depicted as a heavenly messenger and, perhaps, librarian. In another legend from the *Aggadah*, Moses is told that he has one more day to live on Earth, so he writes out the Torah on 13 scrolls, 12 for the 12 tribes and one to keep in the holy Ark of the Covenant as a benchmark, in case anyone tampers with the other 12. When Moses becomes anxious about the amount of time he has left, God slows down the sun, so that it will not set until the task is complete. At last, Moses hands out the scrolls to the tribes, instructing them to keep the commandments. Then Gabriel takes the most beautiful scroll and carries it through the heavens to the highest court, so that all celestial beings can witness Moses's piety. Later in the story, Gabriel is one of the archangels who comforts Moses as he is dying: Gabriel arranges a couch for him and Michael drapes it with a purple garment.

Visions of Gabriel today

Angels and archangels are pure light, and any impression of a physical form that we see in our visualisations can be affected by our expectations. If we have been told that a certain archangel is a particular colour, or carries a particular symbol such as a sword or a pair of scales, we may well see these attributes in our vision. So if you think your inner cinema screen is presenting you with images that you have already seen in paintings or read about (as happened to me when I was seeking to meet Gabriel), ask the archangel to appear to you in a way that is true to its essence. The deeper your meditative state, the more direct your experience of the archangel's essence will be.

MY VISION OF GABRIEL

When I finally met Gabriel he was much less human in appearance than Sandalphon. He was hovering in a brilliant blue sky and seemed to have no feet. His gown was a breathtaking white that sparkled as though made of some kind of crystal. The feathers on his wings vibrated in an even rhythm, occasionally flashing in different colours – mostly blues, greens and turquoise – as though light was shining on them through a prism. A halo of shining golden light radiated from his head. He held a scroll in one hand and from his mouth poured a stream of golden shapes, which seemed to be words and letters in languages I did not recognise. I heard music that sounded like a flute and words were being sung by invisible choirs some- where above. In his other hand Gabriel held a huge shining globe and I could see my own face reflected back to me in its mirrorlike surface.

The constantly flowing stream of words and music fascinated me: I felt I might be able to move into the flow and channel the music and the words and then communicate them myself. Later, I found that I actually could channel messages in this way.[29]

GABRIEL HELPS WITH COMMUNICATION

Jacqueline was asked by her company to train a group of new employees, something she had never done. Despite being taught some training techniques, she was quite apprehensive about delivering this presentation at the end of the week. After a deep meditation Jacqueline decided to put the fear thoughts aside and concentrate fully on the presentation. On the actual day she medi- tated on the image of Gabriel from the *Angels' Script* cards and asked the Archangel Gabriel to accompany her throughout the presentation.

She felt surprisingly calm, firmly believing that Archangel Gabriel was supporting her. The audience was transfixed during the whole presentation, and at the end the training manager commented that

Jacqueline looked as if she had been training for years. Interestingly, he said it was 'as if she held a huge presence around her'. Needless to say, Jacqueline thanked Archangel Gabriel immensely for his assistance. Nowadays she has absolutely no hesitation in standing in front of people and giving presentations and talks. Archangel Gabriel helped her to overcome her habit of convincing herself she couldn't do something, when in fact she could.

Gabriel the modern messenger

Our perception of archangels can change over time. Recently I come across several instances in which Gabriel has updated his means of transport. In Salley Vickers's novel *Mr Golightly's Holiday*, Gabriel travels by motorbike. When I read this I had already been working on my own children's story in which Gabriel buzzes around like a courier on a scooter. Shortly afterwards I held a workshop in Cheltenham; during the meditation one lady saw Gabriel on a motorbike – she described him taking off his helmet and shaking out his long golden hair. Finally, in a futuristic book called *The Traveller* by John Twelve Hawkes, two brothers, Gabriel and Michael, can travel through different dimensions. The government wants to harness their abilities, and Gabriel rides a powerful motorbike in order to evade being tracked on the government's grid.

Calling on Gabriel

Gabriel helps us to develop our ability to receive and communicate messages from the celestial realms. He brings us messages all the time – but do we listen? He is a herald of change and his warnings can help us to adjust so that a change becomes an opportunity and not a crisis. Gabriel helps you organise and make sense of your emotions and beliefs.

Before you work with the Gabriel visualisation, ask yourself these questions:

❖ Are you able to communicate clearly when asking for what you need, or explaining a problem you have?

❖ Have you developed an inner dialogue in which you talk yourself out of getting what you really want?

❖ Have you noticed angelic hints that you need to change things in your life? And are you resisting this idea?

Working with Gabriel will help you develop clarity of mind and the ability to communicate wisely.

Your journey to meet Archangel Gabriel

For a few days before going on this journey, start gathering together items that will remind you of Gabriel's energy: blue, green or turquoise fabrics, a suitable gemstone and a coloured and/or scented candle. Find quotations that speak personal messages to you, especially if you have come across them recently – and also words that have always appealed to you; they can be from poems, psalms, prayers or popular songs. Be light-hearted in your quest, and ask Gabriel inwardly to help you find suitable materials.

Pre-record the visualisation on pages 52–3, or download it from www.workingwitharchangels.com, and follow the instructions for beginning your session. Here are the words to speak to Gabriel (to be included in your recording):

Gabriel, messenger and guide, please let me feel your presence in my life so that I can understand the best path to take, the best decisions to make.

Help me to listen to the messages you bring and understand the signs that are around me every day, so that I can act wisely in the world.

Please tell me if there are any changes I can make that will improve the quality of my life. Help me communicate my needs and hopes to others and encourage me to listen to their needs, so that we can be mutually supportive.

If you have a gift for me to help me on my way, I am willing to receive it into my life.

Come gently out of your meditation in the usual way, and recite the following invocation. Then send the light to anyone who may need angelic help before blowing out your candle.

INVOCATION TO GABRIEL

Gabriel, archangel and messenger of divine intelligence, I am open to guidance and ask you to provide me with the information I need for my spiritual journey. I am travelling on a path that sometimes seems winding and complicated: please bring clarity and insight. I am willing to change in order to move forward.

Other ways to bring Gabriel into your life

❖ Create an icon of Gabriel, collecting suitable pictures and words, or copy the invocation to Gabriel and decorate it with a collage of pictures. Use coloured fabric, feathers, and cut-outs from magazines. Put your finished icon where you can see it while you are working with Gabriel.

❖ There are many famous paintings of Gabriel; see how many you can find. You could go to a gallery near you to look for one.

❖ Keep your journal by your bed. Before you go to sleep, ask Gabriel to send you a message in a dream. As soon as you wake in the morning write down anything that arrives in your head. Even if you don't remember a dream, you will find helpful and beautiful words appearing on the page in front of you. This technique allows you to access the deep realms of divine wisdom in your own heart and mind. The more often you do it the more celestial messages will arrive in your life.

❖ Consider how you communicate with the people you meet every day. Observe how quickly you react and whether you sometimes say things that are not helpful. Resolve always to consider what and how you communicate. Remember the old adage: 'If you can't say anything nice, don't say anything at all.'

❖ Read out loud some old-fashioned poetry – the kind that has rhyme and rhythm – and notice how certain words and phrases affect your emotions.

❖ Join a class to improve your communication skills – a practical course in business correspondence, a creative writing group, a public speaking course, or one on how to talk to children and teenagers.

❖ Listen to music that you feel is divinely inspired, whether classical or popular modern music.

❖ Look at your lifestyle and consider whether any changes are needed. Have you been getting messages and failing to act on them?

If you want to improve your life, it is essential to improve your communications with other people – friends, family and colleagues – but first you must be sure that your own inner conversations are honest; self-deception naturally leads to poor communication with the outer world. For example, don't try to persuade yourself that you don't want something that is really important to you because you think you don't deserve it. Gabriel can help you to uncover your own true desires and to act on them: he will work with your Guardian Angel to remind you what you are really here for.

Summary 1: Sandalphon, Auriel and Gabriel

The three archangels you have met so far can all help you with issues that go back to your early childhood, when the foundations of your life were laid. When we are very small we gather impressions about the world from our environment, which includes the people who bring us up, other children and teachers. These impressions help to form our idea of our individuality and how we can get on in the world. If your life is less successful than you would like it to be, or if you feel unable to express your true self, then you can turn to these archangels at any time to untangle old emotional problems and establish a new sense of confidence.

Archangel Sandalphon will be your ally if you find it difficult to trust that the universe will provide for your needs. If there was a sense of shortage in your childhood, or you were limited by financial hardship – for example, if you wanted to play the piano but your family couldn't afford lessons – Sandalphon will reassure you. His brotherly support will lead you to realise that you can ask for what you need and it will be given to you.

Archangel Auriel will support you if you experienced a lack of tenderness from the people who were nurturing you – perhaps your mother was always busy, or possibly ill, and had no time for you. Perhaps a beloved grandparent died. Auriel's loving energy will cradle you, so that you no longer feel lonely or unlovable. She will help you develop a strong sense of self-worth.

Together, Auriel and Sandalphon help you to create your own perfect 'kingdom', which you can share with everyone.

Archangel Gabriel will help you to see what changes you need to make in your life, and how to communicate your needs clearly. As a child, did you find it difficult to ask for what you wanted? Perhaps you knew the family purse was tight, so you didn't make a fuss about the piano lessons you desperately wanted, and now you have a habit of not asking and not getting. Gabriel's task is to help us think clearly and express our individuality in the world. We can do this through words, music, dance or making pictures. Our relationships in the world, and therefore our success as individuals, depend on communication. This is why Gabriel's *sefira* is called Foundation.

Hanael: the Warrior

Also spelt: Haniel, Aniel
May be the same archangel as Hadraniel,
Kemuel and Chamuel

O God of battles, steel my soldiers' hearts
Possess them not with fear. Take from them now
The sense of rec'ning, ere th'opposed numbers
Pluck their hearts from them.
WILLIAM SHAKESPEARE

Sefira:	Victory
Keywords:	Energy, direction, purpose, assertiveness, vitality
Colours:	All shades of red
Gemstone:	Sardius
Flower remedy:	Impatiens
Essential oil:	Ginger
Planet:	Mars

About Hanael

Hanael's name means 'he who sees God', or 'the glory of God', and he watches over the *sefira* called Victory.

Traditionally Hanael is associated with the planet Venus and the goddess Ishtar. However, this strikes me as incongruous, since Hanael's *sefira* is Victory, and appears on the active, masculine side of the Tree of Life. As you will see, in my own vision I encountered a very lively, assertive energy, which ties in with traditional stories about Hanael, and from my knowledge of astrology he is better linked with Mars.

In ancient mythology, Mars is not only a warrior: he is the god of agriculture, providing the vitality, the spirit of life that encourages the growth of living things. His month is March, when the Spring Equinox occurs and new plants stir after the winter. In the same way, Archangel Hanael encourages new growth and persistence. Think of a small plant pushing up through a concrete pavement – that's Hanael's energy.

Stories concerning Hanael

The name Hanael does not occur in many stories, but according to the well-known angel researcher Gustav Davidson,[30] he is the same character as Kemuel (sometimes spelt Chamuel), meaning 'he who seeks God'.[31] Some stories say that he led the angels who drove Adam and Eve from the Garden of Eden, and along with Gabriel he strengthened Jesus's will in the Garden of Gethsamene the night before his arrest.

Moses challenges the Archangels

Kemuel appears in a legend[32] about Moses in the wilderness that takes place after God has revealed himself to Moses on Mount Sinai. On that particular day God extended time, so that the sun never set, and at the end of this long day God invited Moses to visit Him in heaven. A cloud appeared – Moses walked through an opening and suddenly found himself walking about in heaven, just as he had been walking on the Earth.

Archangel Kemuel, described as a 'porter' at the gate of heaven and in charge of 12,000 angels, challenged Moses: 'What are you doing here, son of Abraham, on this spot, belonging to angels of fire?' Moses replied that he had permission from the Holy One to be there; he had come to receive the Torah[33] and take it to the Israelites. Kemuel still refused to let Moses by, so the prophet destroyed him. (However, Kemuel still seems to be alive and well!)

Moses continued on his way until he met another archangel

porter, called Hadraniel, a name that means 'majesty of God'. Hadraniel also challenged Moses, roaring: 'What are you doing here, son of Abraham, here on the spot of the Holy and High?' Moses, feeling very sorry for himself, started to cry and nearly fell off the cloud. Finally God intervened, and said to Hadraniel: 'You angels have been quarrelsome since the day I created you.' If the Torah could not be delivered to the children of Israel, said God, the angels would no longer be allowed to live in heaven. Hadraniel was most apologetic and promised to be a humble messenger for Moses and go ahead of him, as a disciple goes ahead of his master. However, when they arrived at the 'fire of Sandalphon', Hadraniel said he would have to turn back in case he was scorched.

After meeting Archangels Sandalphon and Raziel (whom you will read about later), Moses eventually received the Torah from Archangel Jophiel, the 'prince of the Torah'. All the other angels became friends to Moses and each of them gave him remedies, including a remedy against death. Archangel Metatron also taught him the secret of the Holy Names.

Although Kemuel and Hadraniel appear to be two different characters, in this tale they are both challengers performing the same task – keeping intruders out of heaven. They both seem to be warrior angels. Henry Cornelius Agrippa (the medieval writer on the occult)[34] associates Kemuel with the strength of Samson, the biblical strongman who was able to kill a young lion with his bare hands.

It is often the case in celestial stories that an archangel will have more than one name – for example, in this story Jophiel and Metatron are different archangels, but elsewhere Jophiel is a name given to Metatron himself.[35] The name 'Aniel' is part of Hadraniel's name, and I have come to the conclusion that these similarities may mean that we can call on any of these names – Hanael, Aniel, Hadraniel or Kemuel – as long as we are clear about the divine attribute we are hoping to access. Will power and consistency of purpose are qualities that we can access when we work with Hanael.

Visions of Hanael today

Despite his warrior-like connotations, the Hanael that I met on my own journey was quite an abstract image.

MY VISION OF HANAEL

I saw a very tall, spinning cone coloured very deep pink and cherry red. The cone rose from a narrow base and then circled out in brilliant, glowing coils into a wide disc that had shining spokes. The disc rotated in a persistent rhythm but occasionally changed its angle, so that sometimes I could only see the flat edge of the disc and at other times I saw a two-dimensional mandala. From this first cone another, much slimmer, gyrating cone rose upwards to become a very fine red line, so that I began to have the impression of an arm holding a sword, but I couldn't really see a figure.

There was a gently shifting aura of very deep pink that seemed featherlike, and vague shapes that might have been fine cloth undulating as the cones turned. I was reminded of the Sufi dervishes who hold floating cloths that move up and down as they whirl on one spot. There was music in the background, with a regular beat from an instrument that sounded rather like a tabor or a bodran, and there was constant movement, tremendous energy and vitality. I had the feeling that this energy was so persistent and demanding that nothing could interrupt its flow.

Much later I realised, with some amusement, that Hanael reminded me of the Red Queen in *Alice Through the Looking Glass* – always on the move, running to stand still. I also thought of some lines by Dylan Thomas: 'The force that drives the water through the rocks/ Drives my red blood . . .'[36]

When I began giving workshops on angels and archangels, the participants mostly wanted to work with gentle, kindly angels, especially the better known ones like Raphael. The sterner Hanael and Samael were not top of the popularity poll. However, this situation has gradually changed as my students understand the value of the energies these archangels provide. Susannah, for example, has been studying with me for some time.

HANAEL HELPS SUSANNAH'S SALES FIGURES

Susannah works under a great deal of pressure in a supervisory role in a busy environment. Her company demands a great deal from its staff and she often works very late and has to give up family time at weekends. Susannah has been doing SoulSchool courses for several years and makes no secret of the fact that she relies on help from archangels when she is feeling stressed. She gets plenty of witty comments about her belief that the archangels will help her out, but she takes it all with good humour, pointing out that she copes with the pressure better than the jokers.

Often the pressure to achieve sales targets is very intense. One particular day Susannah arrived at work feeling pretty fed up, and everyone else was gloomy at the prospect of the difficult day ahead. Susannah announced to her colleagues that she was going to call in Hanael to help lift their vitality and determination. She explained that Hanael was the archangel who could help them all become upbeat in their presentation, and assertive without being over-the-top pushy. This idea was greeted with hilarity, but at least that changed the mood. The energy in the office shifted immediately, everybody got into action with plenty of will and vivacity and by the end of the afternoon their targets had been achieved and even exceeded. As Susannah pointed out, Archangel Hanael had helped them achieve the end result. The staff left feeling very successful, even if some were still sceptical.

Calling on Hanael

When would you want to call on this energetic archangel? Hanael provides us with the drive to activate our choices. Whenever things are getting you down or you feel low in spirits, Hanael's vitality will bring a new perspective and help you recharge your batteries. Before meeting him, ask yourself the following questions:

❖ Are you angry? Does your anger appear as open aggression or do you harbour inner resentments and grudges?
❖ Are you a victim? What prevents you from using your energy to get what you want in life?
❖ Can you be assertive without harming yourself or others?

Hanael will help you direct your energy towards the best possible goals, and will support you when you commit to fulfilling your destiny.

Your journey to meet Archangel Hanael

For a few days before going on this journey, start collecting items that will remind you of Hanael's energy: red or deep pink fabrics, a red candle, a red gemstone. Consider how 'warrior' energy can be used for positive ends. Perhaps you could find a picture of someone who persistently stood up for their beliefs – a good female example is Emily Pankhurst, who was defiant in her pursuit of votes for women. Another woman who was a teenage heroine of mine is Gladys Aylward, who accompanied a troupe of small Chinese children across the mountains to save them from the invading Japanese during the Second World War.[37]

You might also listen to a recording of a famous speech – perhaps Martin Luther King's famous 'I have a dream', or Winston Churchill's 'We will fight on the beaches . . . we will never surrender . . .', or Henry V's Battle of Agincourt speech from Shakespeare's play 'Once more unto the breach, dear friends . . .'

Pre-record the visualisation on pages 52–3, or download it from www.workingwitharchangels.com, and follow the instructions for beginning your session. Here are the words to speak to Hanael (to be included in your recording):

Hanael, encourage me to keep focused on my goals, and be my cheerleader when my energy is low.
Please suggest any changes to my lifestyle that will increase my vitality and my enthusiasm.

> *If my energy is in any way being misdirected please tell me, and show me ways to be wholehearted in my commitment to my true destiny.*
>
> *If you have a symbolic gift for me to help me on my way, I am willing to receive it into my life.*

After coming out of your meditation in the usual way, speak the following invocation to Hanael. Then send the light to anyone needing angelic help, before blowing out your candle.

INVOCATION TO HANAEL

Hanael, warrior archangel, watch over and encourage me when I am feeling weak. Help me to assert my own needs without trespassing on the rights of others. I wish to use my drive for achievement creatively, for the greater good. Please show me how to use my warrior energy and my anger to positive ends.

Other ways to bring Hanael into your life

❖ Create an icon. Copy the invocation to Hanael on an A4 piece of card, and around it make a collage of pictures that remind you of Hanael's energy. Include images of heroic people you admire. Put your finished icon where you can see it while you are working with Hanael.

❖ Consider how you can use your own warrior energy to improve your life. Practise asserting your needs with good grace. Is there something you have wanted to say to someone, but have been too anxious to speak up? It's time to be honest and say clearly what needs to be said.

❖ Is it time to state your needs at work? Ask for a pay rise. Tidy the dusty shelf that no one else seems to notice, buy a new plant for it and suggest that people share responsibility for making the office a good place to work in.

❖ Do you feel strongly about an injustice, but haven't so far acted on it? Find a 'battle' to fight – perhaps the local school is campaigning against a proposed mobile phone mast that will overshadow the playground. Stand up for your rights, and help others to do the same.

❖ Watch a film about a hero or heroine who persists against the odds. It doesn't have to be a war film: you could choose a story about a long trek across the ice or through the jungle, or a space journey – *Apollo 13* is a good movie, famous for the catchphrase 'failure is not an option'.

❖ Physical vitality is a hallmark of Hanael energy, so get walking, running or dancing.

❖ Try hitting a punch ball! Or play a game of tennis. Take a lesson in martial arts, fencing or archery.

❖ Wear something red for a week.

❖ Choose some new goals for your life and set yourself a target for a 'specific measurable result' to achieve within a certain timeframe. Whenever you feel inadequate to a task, ask Hanael for a boost.

Whenever you are feeling weak or depressed, remember Hanael and do something that will liven up your fighting spark. Don't allow yourself to feel downtrodden, and don't think that your opinions or needs don't matter – stand up for yourself. Be clear who you are, then do what you have to do in order to live your life to the full. Hanael's dynamic energy is available to all of us. Make conscious choices about how you will use your share of this power. Victory is not about beating other people, but about remaining in command of yourself.

Raphael: the Healer

Also spelt: Rafael. Other names: Boel and Labbiel

Raphael, the sociable spirit that deigned
To travel with Tobias, and secured
His marriage with the seven-times wedded maid.
JOHN MILTON

Sefira:	Splendour
Keywords:	Reassurance, harmony, reconciliation, healing, love
Colours:	Pink, lilac, lavender
Gemstone:	Amethyst
Flower remedy:	Centaury
Essential oil:	Lavender
Planet:	Venus

About Raphael

Raphael's name means 'healing of God'. He (or she) is always included in the various different lists of seven Archangels of the Presence and is well known as one of the four Archangels of the Directions who watch over Creation.

There are conflicting ideas about which planet Raphael can be associated with. Some occult traditions say the Sun, others Mercury. But Michael is often identified as the Archangel of the Sun, which is appropriate for the 'commander in chief' (see Michael, p. 99), and I believe Gabriel is equally right as archangel for Mercury. As Raphael is on the passive, feminine, side of the Tree of Life, described as a diplomat and rescuer in the Creation story, and as a healer and matchmaker in the Book of Tobit, I think it is quite appropriate to assign Raphael to the planet Venus.

Stories concerning Raphael

A major story in the *Aggadah* supports this suggestion. When King Solomon wanted to build his temple, Raphael gave him a ring engraved with a pentagram, a five-pointed star,[38] which gave Solomon power over all the demons so that he could put them to work. The five-pointed star is a symbol for Venus, whose transit through the heavens appears from the Earth to create a pattern of five equal loops.[39] In the astrological tradition, Venus brings people together in every kind of social relationship. Confidence and joy in personal relationships is a powerful aspect of the healing process. Men can, obviously, be very good healers, but I always think of Raphael as feminine.

In an old Creation legend found in the *Aggadah*, Raphael is at first called Labbiel. When God decided to create the Earth and humans to live on it, he consulted his angels. This, the story tells us, demonstrates that God is modest and sets an example to human beings, however great, not to scorn advice from the humble and lowly. But the angels were divided: the angel of love favoured the creation of human beings, as they would be affectionate and loving. The angel of truth opposed it, as humans would be full of lies. The angel of justice was in favour, as humans would practise justice. The angel of peace was against, because humans would be quarrelsome.

Had the angels known all the facts about humans, the story continues, they would have objected even more strongly, but God only told them about the best of human possibilities. Even so, Archangel Michael and his hosts were against the creation of humanity, and so were Gabriel and his angels. God stretched forth his little finger and all the hosts of angels commanded by these two great archangels vanished, leaving only Gabriel and Michael behind.

Archangel Labbiel was wiser, and warned his angels not to go against God. So they all agreed that it would be a great idea to create humans, and promised to minister to their needs and share their secrets with them. Then God changed Labbiel's name to Raphael (translated in this story as 'the rescuer'), and appointed him the angel of healing who has in his safe-keeping all the medical remedies that can be used on Earth. In the *Zohar*, Raphael is on watch during the morning hours and brings relief to the sick and suffering. He cured Jacob's thigh, which had been injured when Jacob wrestled with an angel, and soothed the pain when Moses was circumcised.

In this legend, even though God is modest enough to consult the angels, He does not want to take their advice; they are jealous of human beings because God made humans superior to all other creatures. The author explains that this is because only humans have sprung from the hand of God, while the rest of Creation sprang from the word of God. Also, each human is a microcosm, a miniature of the whole world, and both heavenly and earthly qualities are united in each one of us.

Tobias and the Angel

The most famous legend concerning Raphael is found in the Book of Tobit, written around the 2nd century BC.[40] This delightful tale demonstrates Raphael's task as a healer both of the physical body and of relationships.

Tobias lived in Nineveh, the capital city of Assyria,[41] with his father Tobit. Unable to work after losing his sight, Tobit had become very poor. He prayed for help, God heard him and a divine plan was set in motion.

Recalling that he had lent ten silver talents to a man who lived some distance away in Medea, Tobit asked his son Tobias to go and reclaim the money. The journey would be dangerous and Tobit advised Tobias to go into Nineveh to find a guide. Very quickly Tobias met a pilgrim called Brother Azarias, who agreed to accompany him. Tobias had no idea that the 'pilgrim' was the Archangel Raphael, sent by God to help his family. The journey took the two travellers by a river, where Azarias told Tobias to catch a fish, which made them a good lunch. Then he instructed Tobias to save the heart, liver and gall of the fish for future use.

In the meantime, in Medea, a young woman called Sarah was also praying – for a husband. She had already married seven times, but in each case before the newlyweds could get into their marriage bed a demon had arrived and frightened away the groom. God instructed Raphael to help her as well.

When Tobias arrived in Medea his 'guide' took him to meet Sarah's family, who – by divine coincidence – were related to Tobias. Azarias announced that Sarah would make Tobias a good wife, but the young man had heard about the demon and was not at all keen. Azarias reassured him that the demon could be thwarted: Tobias must take the heart and liver of the fish, lay them on incense and burn the ingredients in the bridal chamber. The demon would smell the smoke and run away, never to return. The archangel's ruse was successful, and Tobias and Sarah were married. Azarias attended their wedding feast, telling them later that, being an angel, he had had to create the illusion he was eating. Tobias received a rich dowry, and also reclaimed his father's money.

The newlyweds travelled home, where Raphael (still disguised as Azarias) gave Tobias a recipe for an ointment to be made from a fish's gallbladder. Tobias used the ointment on his father's eyes, and immediately his cataracts fell away and he could see again. At the celebratory feast Tobias offered Azarias half the money he had brought back – much more than the promised fee. It was only then that the archangel revealed himself in his true form, as Raphael. Then Raphael ascended back to God, after instructing the happy family to write their story in a book (Tobit 1–12).[42]

Visions of Raphael today

MY VISION OF RAPHAEL
When I asked to meet Raphael the only image I had was from my art history studies showing the archangel in pilgrim's garb,

wingless and not at all ethereal. I did know that Raphael was 'the Healer', but I didn't really know what to expect when I went on my inner journey. My first impression of Archangel Raphael was of very delicate colours: lilac, lavender and soft pink. Soft, wispy, cloudlike textures floated around me and I had a sensation of being wrapped in a light-as-thistledown garment by someone who was caring and compassionate. I could hear music that sounded like an Aeolian harp, a stringed instrument that stands outside and allows the gentlest of breezes to brush its strings. When I looked for a face I saw a shining head crowned with pink roses; the eyes were closed and the eyelashes were golden rays streaming downwards. The lilac colours merged into a haze of wings and feathers and the pink became a shining ribbon on which floated the words: 'I am the river of Divine Healing, flowing over the Earth.'

Amethyst and rose pink are very good colours for healing – crystal healers use them a lot – so these are very suitable colours for Raphael. Some books suggest green, but I associate green with change – obviously healing involves change, so you may be quite comfortable with green for Raphael. I always tell my students not to just accept what they find in books, but to experiment and see what works best for them.

A HEALING DREAM OF RAPHAEL

One of my students, Anya, works for a global organisation whose aim is to reduce poverty in Third World countries. She is frustrated by the bureaucracy entailed in her work and feels her energy is not really being used for the benefit of poor people, but rather to sustain the organisation. She told me that she felt Raphael as a warm, comforting and loving energy that enabled her to redirect her thoughts, in a very vivid dream. In her dream Anya saw Raphael smiling at her, asking her how she felt about 'the present situation'. She knew the archangel was referring to her work and responded immediately by telling Raphael that it was difficult, discouraging and not bringing positive results. She went on to say that she was struggling with the challenges and did not feel rewarded for all the long hours she was spending at the office.

Raphael listened without comment, but as she continued to complain, Anya felt that she had to stop and start focusing on the positive aspects of her work. She found herself saying things like, 'I am given great opportunities to learn and grow professionally,' and 'All these challenges are actually good for me.' She felt a significant directional change, as if she was a wheel turning through 180 degrees. It was as though the very presence of the archangel had allowed her to perceive her life in a completely new way. Anya does not usually remember her dreams, but this one was so powerful that she recalled it several times that day.

Anya's dream reminds us how important it is to notice how we think about our lives and re-evaluate our judgements. We can choose to see the cloud – or the silver lining inside it.

Calling on Raphael

You don't have to be ill to call on Raphael – although she is a powerfully ally for anyone facing an operation or invasive medical treatment. Raphael encourages us to open our hearts to the world, enabling us to empathise with others, so that our relationships flourish and in turn our own hurts dissolve. If your relationships are fraught with emotional difficulties, Raphael will bring a soothing balm; she is a diplomat as well as a matchmaker. She encourages us to appreciate and respect others and ourselves equally – the motto 'do as you would be done by' could have been written by Raphael. Remember, too, that in the story of Tobias, along with the marriage and the healing came the restoration of wealth. In order to succeed in the material world we need good relationships and the willing exchange of our gifts and talents.

Before meeting Raphael, ask yourself the following questions:

❖ Do you feel unloved and unlovable?

❖ Are you able to share with other people – your joys as well as your negative feelings? Or are you emotionally inhibited?

❖ Do you suffer from a physical or emotional disability?

❖ Do you feel hard up and hard done by?

Raphael will help you unwind your tensions and anxieties, allowing you to release your resistance to divine healing. Whether our pain is emotional or physical, when we let go it dissolves. When we are emotionally and physically healthy, we can also be confident of our material well-being.

Your journey to meet Archangel Raphael

For a few days before going on this journey, start gathering together items that will remind you of Raphael's energy: soft pink or lilac fabrics or feathers, a pink candle, and pink and lilac flowers, especially roses. Lavender has a very soothing essence, so find a lavender room spray or some dried lavender. Choose your own collection of floral perfumes. Interestingly, there are a lot of pink products on the market today – even tool sets for your car. Perhaps Raphael is provoking us to 'think pink' and ease up on some of our grey thoughts!

Raphael holds the energy for the *sefira* Splendour, also translated as Glory, and she brings a gentle but very powerful radiance with her. Think about people you know or know of who have a natural ability to soothe troubled waters. When we work with Raphael we glow with radiant energy and this allows other people to unwind. In the words of one of my husband Will's songs it is 'easy, peasy . . . love is the key to understanding'. You could listen to this song on www.soulschool.co.uk, or perhaps to the Beatles singing 'All you need is love'.

You may find yourself quite tearful during or after this journey, as Raphael shifts old emotional blocks. Have a box of tissues handy, as well as a glass of water with some Rescue Remedy, before making yourself comfortable and listening to your tape.

Pre-record the visualisation on pages 52–3, or download it from www.workingwitharchangels.com, and follow the instructions for beginning your session. Here are the words to speak to Raphael (to be included in your recording):

> *Raphael, help me open my heart so that I can give love freely and receive love in return.*
>
> *Heal my old emotional wounds and encourage my physical body to heal itself so that every cell in my body becomes radiant with divine energy.*
>
> *Remind me that my material welfare is assured and that I can let go of negative responses, like resentment, envy and fear.*
>
> *Allow me to bring your splendour into the lives of all those I meet, especially those who feel poor and unloved.*
>
> *If you have a symbolic gift for me to help me on my way, I am willing to receive it into my life.*

When you have completed the visualisation, speak the following invocation to Raphael, remembering to send light to anyone who may need angelic help before you blow out your candle.

INVOCATION TO RAPHAEL

Raphael, archangel and divine healer, I understand that divine love heals all things and I open myself to the flow of this love. I seek healing for myself, and the inspiration to heal others I meet. Remind me, day by day, that we are all connected, and help me to unblock the channels through which love can flow into my life.

Other ways to bring Raphael into your life

❖ Create a visual reminder of Raphael by using your art materials, collages, quotations or other images. Keep it where you will notice it in the morning and evening.

❖ Consider how you can use your own healing energy in everyday ways – just a smile to a passing stranger who is looking anxious can make a difference to their day.

❖ Get involved in a local group that promotes understanding between people who seem to have irreconcilable differences.

❖ Think about why people commit crimes or acts of terror and try to understand why they behave in this way. Raphael does not require you to overlook or forgive human wickedness, but to understand its roots and work towards healing the pain that causes negative behaviour.

❖ Think of something fun to do with someone you love. A simple activity is best – go for a walk, go the park with a ball, fly a kite.

❖ Give yourself a loving treat. Include something pink. A bubble bath scented with roses is very Raphael!

❖ Offer to visit someone in hospital who has no close family or friends.

❖ Take pleasure in your own material possessions; enjoy beautiful things – trees, flowers, clouds, stars, paintings, buildings, statues – and give thanks for them.

❖ Enjoy being in your physical body – dance, skip, skate – whatever 'turns you on'.

Whenever you are feeling hard done by or lonely, remind yourself of Raphael's loving energy. Don't feel sorry for yourself. The world is a glorious place to be, so thank the universe for being there for all of us: say 'thank you' when you get up in the morning, and when you go to bed at night.

Michael: the Leader

Islamic spelling: Mika'il. Also called Shabbatiel

Angel, king of streaming morn;
Cherub, call'd by Heav'n to shine;
Guide aetherial, power divine;
Thou Lord of all within!
HENRY ROWE

Sefira:	Beauty
Keywords:	Courage, commitment, honour, faith, protection
Colours:	Gold, sunshine yellow, red
Gemstone:	Carbuncle
Flower remedy:	Cerato
Essential oil:	Angelica
Planet:	The Sun

About Michael

Michael's name means 'he who is like God'. In ancient Persian lore Michael was called Beshtar, 'one who provides sustenance for mankind', and he is often called the Archangel of the Sun. Another name for him is Shabbatiel, meaning 'rest of God' (Shabbat is the Jewish day of rest). Jewish, Christian and Islamic traditions all hold him in the highest esteem.

In many paintings Michael is depicted wearing a cloak lined with red because he was considered to be a seraph. Although some occult writers give Michael the colour blue, I suggest that blue is too cool for this shining archangel, who radiates the glory of God into the world. Michael represents the best in leadership; he is a protective archangel and is the patron saint of policemen. He is also often shown holding a pair of scales in which to weigh the souls of the dead.

Stories concerning Michael

Michael has been called the Herald of Death because he was sent by God to warn both Abraham and Mary, the mother of Jesus, that they would have to leave their earthly lives. In one of the *Aggadah* stories Michael is the angel who appears in the burning bush.

Muslim lore says that Michael lives in the seventh heaven, surrounded by an 'innumerable array of angels', that his wings are the colour of emeralds and that 'he is covered with saffron hairs, each of them containing a million faces and mouths and as many tongues which, in a million dialects, implore the pardon of Allah'.[43]

In the legend *The Testament of Abraham*,[44] Michael arrived on Earth to find Abraham in a field he was about to plough. Taking Michael to be a stranger, Abraham offered Michael a ride on one of his animals, but Michael told him that he never rode on four-footed creatures. As they walked together past a tree, Abraham heard a voice singing 'Holy art thou, because thou hast kept the purpose for which thou wast sent.' Abraham thought that he was the only one to hear the voice, but later, when he offered to wash the stranger's feet, he suddenly found himself weeping, and then his son Isaac also started to weep. Even Archangel Michael shed tears, which fell into the basin of water and became precious stones.

Then Michael flew to heaven in the twinkling of an eye, to explain to God that he could not bring himself to tell Abraham he was going to die. God told Michael to return and pretend to have a meal with his host. Then, when everyone was asleep, God would send Isaac a dream warning him that his father was going to die.

Unfortunately, when the dream was related to Abraham he refused to go to heaven. So Michael had to go and tell God the bad news. God was very patient and Michael was sent down again, this time with a message reminding Abraham that God had sent the chief archangel for his companion on the journey to heaven, which should be regarded as a great privilege. Nevertheless, Abraham bargained with Michael: he wanted to be taken up in his body, so that he could see all Creation as he left the Earth. So Michael was allowed to take Abraham on a chariot surrounded by cherubim and they looked down on the Earth, seeing both the good and the bad. But still Abraham resisted his death, even after God had taken Michael off the case and sent Death with his sickle. Eventually God took Abraham's soul while he was sleeping and Michael took it up to heaven.

This ancient legend gives us plenty of clues about Michael, who is compassionate towards Abraham, and appreciates the patriarch's holy nature. Like Raphael in the story of Tobias, Michael arrives as a stranger and neither Abraham nor his son Isaac recognises him as an archangel; also like Raphael, he has to trick the humans into believing that he is eating and drinking with them. Michael driving the heavenly chariot through the sky is reminiscent of legends of Sun gods.

The prophet Daniel had a vision of Michael, as well as of Gabriel. After fasting for three days Daniel saw a 'man clothed in linen' with a body of beryl and limbs of burnished bronze.[45] This archangel, who was probably Gabriel, told Daniel that Michael, 'one of the chief princes', had been helping to overcome the princes of Persia (Daniel 10.13). Although there were many years of turmoil ahead, Michael would protect the people of Israel and deliver them from their enemies (Daniel 12.1). These chapters in the Book of Daniel suggest that each nation has its own archangel, described as a 'prince' (which may be why Pseudo-Dionysius thought that there were 'princedoms' in heaven). One of the Dead Sea Scrolls, entitled *The War of the Sons of Light against the Sons of Darkness*, mentions Michael as the 'Prince of Light'.

The most famous story about Michael appears in the Book of Revelation describing his battle with the Devil (in the form of a serpent) and his supporters (told in Chapter 2, p. 22). Hundreds of churches in England are still named after Michael and all his angels, in which Michael is often portrayed slaying the serpent. A golden statue of Michael shines on the top of Mont St Michel in France, and if you go to St Michael's Mount in Cornwall, you will find a modern statue of him by Jill Constable Maxwell, stretching out his hand to the Devil in a gesture of reconciliation.

Visions of Michael today

As I mentioned earlier, to meet the archangels I would visualise the Tree of Life as a tall building and imagine myself going up in a lift. When the lift door opened I would see before me a corridor and a door, and I would ask to meet the archangel behind the door. I soon discovered that I had to enter – the archangel would not come out to me!

MY VISION OF MICHAEL

When I entered the corridor that led me to Michael's door, I found myself in complete darkness, black and velvety. Then the 'door' appeared, a magnificent portal shining with bright colours, as though studded with brilliant jewels. I walked into an area like a vast hall, with luminous, transparent walls, although they had some feeling of solidity. I felt as though I was in a cathedral, a building with a roof so high that it disappeared into the heavens. Light poured in through invisible windows and moved downwards in delicate rays and criss-cross shafts at quite a speed, like a laser show. I heard singing; I could not tell whether it came from a single voice or a choir of thousands. There was no real melody and the notes hardly changed – I would say they hovered around the top few notes of the scale of C.

Michael himself beamed down from high in the vaults of this ethereal building. His 'face' had only a suggestion of features and his wings radiated like flashing rays of sunshine. I was sitting in my usual meditation position on the bed, but mentally I fell on my knees in amazement and wonder.

People with a more musical ear than mine may well pick up a wealth of music when they visit the archangels. I always heard some kind of music when I met them, and I would expect them all to have their own 'song'.

In Chapter 3 you will have read part of the story about Juliet, who was asked by the Archangel Michael to pass on a message from the angels. You will remember that she asked him to provide a confirmation that she wasn't hallucinating. Here is what happened.

ARCHANGEL MICHAEL AND THE CAB DRIVER

On her way to the conference rehearsal, Juliet waited 20 minutes in the cold for a cab, in vain. Then she was struck by what seemed to be a brilliant idea. (In retrospect, she believed the idea was planted by the angelic form that had visited her in the room.) She said aloud: 'Okay, Michael, here's your chance. I've got to get up to the cathedral and I'm running late. Surely in all of Manhattan, you can find one cab that's empty!'

Within minutes, a free cab pulled up and she hopped in. There, stuck onto the dashboard was a large and obviously cheap plastic statue of a winged form that bore the words 'The Right Archangel Michael'. For a moment, Juliet couldn't speak. Even synchronicity seemed unable to explain this incredible 'coincidence'. Juliet stammered to the driver, 'Tell me, what are you doing with the Archangel Michael in your cab?'

The driver, Tony, replied, 'Lady, let me tell you, he's a special friend of mine – he's my best friend Mike! . . . Hey, he's the greatest! Let me tell you, my wife, she gets mad at me, she throws the spaghetti across the kitchen, I call on Mike and ask him, how do you handle women? The kids get in trouble in school, I call on Mike. I can't pay the rent, I call on Mike. I really recommend him to you – he can do anything! Of course I have him in my cab!'

For the whole journey he lectured Juliet on the virtues of the Archangel Michael, and why he was Tony's best and greatest friend. After paying her fare, she told herself, 'All right, Juliet, you asked for a message, and now you've got to keep your promise!'

As you know, Juliet kept her end of the deal, and gave the angelic message in the cathedral. Later, she said, 'I didn't know angels had such a sense of humour. I felt the archangel himself was getting such a kick out of what was going on in that cab.'

Calling on Michael

When would you want to call on this splendid archangel? Ask yourself the following questions:

❖ Do you feel in charge of your own life?
❖ Does fear prevent you from creating a life that you love?
❖ Do you believe that you have a right to be your true self?
❖ Do you honour the divine monarch within yourself and others?

Michael will be your ally when you need the courage to face difficulties. He provides a psychic 'breastplate' and helps you polish your golden armour – the inner armour that strengthens your commitment and faith.

Michael helps you to take charge of your life purpose, gives your spirit courage and confirms your right to self-expression so that you become the commander of your own life.

Your journey to meet Archangel Michael

A few days before your session, look out for objects, stones, jewellery and fabrics that remind you of sunshine – anything golden or sunset red will encourage Michael's energy in your life – and put them on your table. Look for images of Michael. Some ancient icons show him sitting on a splendid throne with scales in his hand – personally I prefer these to the medieval images of him in armour, slaying a devil. Look for images, too, of contemporary or historical people who have drawn on Michael's leadership energy. Use an extra-large golden or yellow candle for Michael, one that makes you think of sunshine.

Michael is a regal figure and helps you gain spiritual sovereignty. Before you start your journey play some royal music that makes you feel splendid. Trumpet music is very suitable, and Handel in particular – *The Entrance of the Queen of Sheba, The Hallelujah Chorus, The Water Music,* for example – will bring a Michael mood into your room. My vision of Michael made me think of the coronation of Queen Elizabeth II in Westminster Abbey and the mass shout of 'Vivat Regina!' ('Long live the Queen!') when the crown was held over her head.

Pre-record the visualisation on pages 52–3, or download it from www.workingwitharchangels.com, and follow the instructions for beginning your session. Here are the words to speak to Michael (to be included in your recording):

Michael, I want to work with you to chase away doubts and anxieties, so that I can lead a life based on courage, commitment and faith.

Fill my heart with your golden light and remind me of it whenever I feel weak.

Let me walk in your beauty and strength and help me to radiate them out into the world, whatever the circumstances.

If you have a symbolic gift for me to help me on my way, I am willing to receive it into my life.

At the end of your journey, recite the following invocation. Then send the light to people around the world who may need angelic help before blowing out the candle.

INVOCATION TO MICHAEL

Michael, archangel and commander over all archangels, open my heart to the true beauty of divine power. Help me to take charge of my spiritual destiny and become the commander of my life. Allow the centre of divine light that resides within me to unfold its radiance and shine in its true light.

Other ways to bring Michael into your life

❖ Create a visual reminder of Michael. Use plenty of glitter, gold paper and gold paint. Write out the invocation with a gold pen and seal it like a royal proclamation with red paint or sealing wax.

❖ Imagine what it feels like to be royal – how would you stand, walk and speak?

❖ Consider how you can honour people you know. Then put your ideas into action as soon as possible.

❖ Rewrite the story about Michael and the Devil, imagining that Michael was determined not to slay the Devil, but to make friends with him. Find some children to read your story to – you could use the story of St George and the Dragon instead, if the children you know aren't into angels.

❖ What makes you scared? Could you try breaking your fear barrier over one thing?

❖ Go somewhere grand – a cathedral, or a museum with big steps.

❖ Play music that stirs courage in your heart.

If ever you are feeling afraid and need courage to go forward in your life, you can turn to Michael. He will help you become the true master of your fate and the captain of your soul.[46]

Summary 2: Hanael, Raphael and Michael

These three archangels all contribute to the spiritual support system we need as we grow up and meet the world beyond our family. When children go to school, they have to learn how to assert themselves without being aggressive (Hanael). They need to develop diplomacy and empathy for others (Raphael). Above all they need to learn to maintain their sense of self and not to fall prey to doubts and fears (Michael). If any of these psychic building blocks were not put in place when you were younger, then work with the archangels to develop them now.

Archangel Hanael will support you whenever you have to assert your needs, both in the workplace and in relationships. His job is to help you survive, emotionally and physically. Another translation of Hanael's *sefira* Victory is 'Endurance': if your energy is flagging he provides the adrenalin for 'the long haul' – such as moving house, a night in a hospital beside a loved one or meeting an important deadline at work.

Archangel Raphael pours oil on troubled waters. We all want to survive, but that has to be achieved as gracefully as possibly. Raphael will gently wash away difficulties between people – providing they are willing to release their old fixations. Remember her role as 'the rescuer': repairing rifts, healing wounds, opening the way to new ways of loving – all these are under Raphael's remit. Since healing does not always mean curing, Raphael eases the process of dying and the grief of those left behind. Her *sefira* is Splendour and she has a gentle sense of self. She knows how to just be, without needing to assert herself; yet she is not passive, but calm and graceful. Work with her to bring these qualities into your psyche.

Archangel Michael encourages you to grow into a self-sufficient, self-aware person who knows their own true destiny and is able to walk their talk without being pompous. When you work with Michael you will be 'clothed with the heavens and crowned with stars and perceive yourself to be the sole heir to the whole world',[47] and you will also learn that there are people in the world 'who are ev'ry one sole heirs as well as you'. Michael aims for individual sovereignty with respect for all. This is the true 'beauty' of his gateway to light – that we should all become monarchs ruling our own lives.

Zadkiel: the Comforter

Also spelt: Tzadkiel; possibly he is also Melchizedek

He maketh me to lie down in green pastures: he leadeth me
by the still waters . . . My cup overflows. Surely goodness
and mercy shall follow me all the days of my life.
PSALM 23:6

Sefira:	Mercy
Keywords:	Abundance, generosity, enthusiasm, comfort
Colours:	Sapphire blue, indigo, violet
Gemstone:	Sapphire
Flower remedy:	Agrimony
Essential oil:	Rosemary
Planet:	Jupiter

About Zadkiel

Zadkiel's name means righteousness of God (*zedek* means right-eousness[48]) and he guards the *sefira* of Mercy. He represents God's benevolence and is included in most lists of the seven archangels who stand before God's throne. In the *Zohar*, Zadkiel is one of two 'chieftains' who carry Archangel Michael's standard when the commander in chief of all angels goes into battle.

Zadkiel holds the energy for the *sefira* Mercy and he represents the willingness to let go of any restriction – think of mercy not only as forgiveness, but also as generosity of heart. Zadkiel provides you with a direct connection to the boundless abundance of the Divine.

Stories concerning Zadkiel

Zadkiel's rulership of the bountiful planet Jupiter is found in all the references I have discovered to this archangel. There are very few old stories that mention Zadkiel by name, but the *Legend of Abraham* mentions that Jupiter shone brightly for the Patriarch the night before he conquered the king of Sodom. After the battle Abraham met a high priest called Melchizedek, who welcomed him with a blessing and a ritual of bread and wine (Genesis 14.18–20). Melchizedek's name contains the word *zedek* and *melech* means 'king', so the priest's name means 'king of righteousness'. He was also king of Salem – *salem* meaning 'peace'. Melchizedek has always had a mysterious reputation. In the New Testament St Paul refers to him as: 'Without father, without mother, without descent, having neither beginning of days, nor end of life; but made like unto the Son of God; abideth a priest continually' (Hebrews 7.3). As a 'Son of God', he may have been Archangel Zadkiel.

Kabbalistic tradition says that the Kabbalah dates back to Abraham, so it is possible that Abraham received it from the mysterious Melchizedek, who would have performed a ritual initiating Abraham into the sacred mysteries.[49] Many of these old stories point to the notion that ancient wisdom was passed down through the generations from a time before the Flood.

Zadkiel and the Comte Saint-Germain

The alchemist Comte Saint-Germain (known in New Age teaching as an 'ascended master') is said to have communicated with Zadkiel. Like Melchizedek, the 'beginnings' of Saint-Germain were unknown, as was his 'end of life'. He was an intriguing figure in European high society during the mid-18th century. An anecdote tells how in 1760 an elderly countess, hearing that a Comte Saint-Germain had been invited to a soirée hosted by Madame de Pompadour, decided to attend herself – she was curious, having met a man of that name in Venice in 1710. When she met the count he assured her that he was the same person. She would not – could not – believe him, because the count she had met in Venice had given his age as 45 and now, 50 years later, this man still appeared to be in his mid-forties. 'Madame, I am very old,' he said, and went on to give convincing details of their earlier meeting.

Among other extraordinary gifts, Saint-Germain had apparently discovered the secret of immortality. Records say that he died in 1784, but throughout the 19th century many people reported meeting him, and said he never aged. He claimed to have personally known the Roman Emperor Nero and to have walked and talked with the Italian Renaissance poet Dante. The 18th-century philosopher Voltaire – respected as a man of science and reason – said: 'He is a man who never dies, and who knows everything.'

Saint-Germain is a popular figure in some New Age teachings. Madame Blavatsky claimed to have met him and other ascended masters, whom the Theosophists believed would help humanity evolve to a higher state of consciousness. Elizabeth Clare Prophet claims that Saint-Germain helped to activate Zadkiel's 'violet flame', a healing energy that will dispel human negativity.

Visions of Zadkiel today

When I set off on my inner journey to meet Zadkiel I knew nothing about Melchizedek and his connections to the priesthood. I did know that Zadkiel is the archangel for Jupiter, who in astrology represents expansion and generosity; this gave me the idea that Zadkiel might be something like St Nicholas, the prototype for Father Christmas, perhaps dressed in ecclesiastical reds and golds. But when I closed my eyes I couldn't even find my usual corridor – I was completely in the dark.

MY VISION OF ZADKIEL
The darkness was cosy and unthreatening, and I could feel soft, velvety walls on each side of me. I groped around trying to find a door, but eventually I gave up – and at that moment a bright white space appeared, like a film screen with only a white light shining

on it. Not sure whether it was solid, I stretched out my hand and found myself sliding through the light, like Alice going through the looking glass. When I emerged I felt as though I had been teleported – I had dissolved in one place and reappeared somewhere else. Everything seemed intact but I felt I was glowing, as though my limbs and clothes had a bright glaze on them.

I seemed to be hanging in deep space. I could hear triumphant music, like a great choir singing. Everything was bright and white, as though I had walked into the reverse of the dark enclosure I had left moments earlier. Some lines from a hymn came into my mind: '. . . in light inaccessible hid from our eyes'. The bright whiteness began to vibrate into curling patterns and I began to shake slightly. The curls rolled all around me, ebbing and flowing like waves. I wanted to say something, but I felt I was in the presence of something or someone so powerful that anything I could ask or say would be meaningless. But then it came to me: 'I think you are wonderful,' I said inwardly.

The curly patterns whirled into a tornado which caught me up, and then I found myself falling through a tunnel of deep purple. The colours were glowing mauve and sapphire blue, almost fluorescent, and I experienced a sensation of silk-satin touching my skin. Eventually I landed on a cushiony floor. The journey was over. I sat with my eyes closed for a few moments, trying to register what I had experienced before I eventually opened my eyes.

Throughout this journey – which was rather like a spiritual roller-coaster ride – there was a sense of expansion and fun. Afterwards I felt totally reassured that the universe is benevolent, and that any restrictions I experienced in my life were self-imposed. I sensed the character of Zadkiel as a jolly grandfather who would give me not just what I 'needed', but also things to make life pleasurable. I was reminded that although we should not be careless, we can be carefree.

Zadkiel often creates abundance by bringing to our attention what we already have. The television programme *Cash in the Attic* reminds me of how he works. The participants choose a goal that requires some cash – for example, a holiday, or refurbishing the kitchen. With the presenter they look around their homes for things they don't want, or hadn't realised were valuable, and then sell them to raise the money. Often people are amazed at discovering the assets they own. Charity shops are also Zadkiel's territory, providing us with great opportunities to give and receive with very little money exchanged.

ZADKIEL CREATES ABUNDANCE FOR A SINGLE MOTHER

Lisa is a single mother in her early thirties. Her daughter Naomi is nearly five and has just started school. Naomi sees other little girls with pretty frocks and often nags her mum for something new to wear. Before her marriage broke up Lisa had dressed Naomi in clothes from good shops and felt it would be a 'come-down' to buy second-hand. But needing to kit Naomi out for the winter term, she followed a friend's advice and went on a charity shop expedition.

Before she set out, Lisa asked Zadkiel to lead her to good-quality clothes in excellent condition: she made a list of what Naomi needed, including the sizes – two white shirts, one navy pullover, one grey skirt and one cosy blue coat. Lisa had a budget of £35 but wanted to keep back around £15 for good-quality new shoes.

Visiting just three charity shops in one street Lisa found all the items she was looking for, and only spent £15. In the last shop she saw a pretty, fairytale frock at £3 that was just the right size for Naomi, so she bought that too. By the end of the day Naomi had her complete uniform, as well as a party frock, for well within Lisa's budget.

One important aspect of this story is that Lisa was very precise about her needs. Having a clear picture in your mind creates a field, rather like a magnet, that attracts your desires into your life.

I hear many stories from people who have been wondering how they were going to cover a bill, or were longing for a relaxing break, when out of the blue something has 'turned up'. Zadkiel encourages us all to share the abundance that we have, and reminds us to be continually grateful for the gifts of Creation.

Calling on Zadkiel

How can this magnificent archangel help you in your everyday life?

The kabbalistic book I used as a reference on my journey says: 'This *sefira* [Mercy] carries the qualities of magnificence, magnanimity and mercy.'[50] Zadkiel's benevolence reminds us that the universe is overflowing with gifts for everyone. His boundless energy encourages us to give and not count the cost, to share what we have and know that what we give comes back to us a thousand-fold, including money.

Zadkiel will help you understand the laws of abundance. Money is like a flowing river; some people create dams so that they can benefit, but that reduces the flow for others. The constant flow of abundance in your life depends on you understanding and using your gifts, and being generous and fearless when it comes to using money. One of Zadkiel's wealth laws is that there will be no shortage.

One of the richest men in the world is the singer-songwriter Bob Dylan. He went to New York when he was a teenager with nothing but a guitar and a few clothes. But, as he has said, he trusted in the benevolence of the universe and in a very short time his trust paid huge dividends. I believe that many unknown people have amazing talents – they are just too frightened to take the risk and go out there, and offer their gifts to the world. What you give comes back to you – that is also one of Zadkiel's laws.

Zadkiel gives you permission to expand your visions and possibilities and adds enthusiasm to the energy of Hanael and the courage of Michael.

Before meeting Zadkiel ask yourself:

❖ Do you feel excited about the possibilities that life offers?
❖ Do you believe that life is joyful and that your success will make it more so, for you and everyone else?

❖ Do you put limits on your imagination when you think about how your life can develop?

❖ Are you able to be generous and magnanimous – not just with money, but in all aspects of life?

Zadkiel will help you to feel a real connection with the boundless abundance of the universe. When you work with his energy you will find yourself spontaneously giving and sharing, not just money and material goods, but compliments, hospitality and time, and you will notice that money, opportunities and gifts flow towards you.

Your journey to meet Archangel Zadkiel

For a few days before going on this journey collect items that will remind you of Zadkiel's energy. If Michael's grandeur reminds us of a monarch, you can think of Zadkiel as the high priest. Purple and gold fabrics, religious icons and artefacts in the Russian Orthodox style would be good. Zadkiel is like Father Christmas bringing gifts for everyone, so you might find suitable decorations in your Christmas tree box. Another festival of lights is Hannukah, during which candles are lit for eight days in succession. This celebrates the time when, after a war in which the Jews struggled to regain their Temple, the one-day supply of oil in the temple lamp lasted for eight days – Zadkiel at work again! You might like to find a seven- or nine-branched menorah or other multiple candle-holder for your Zadkiel table.

Play music that provides a ceremonial or holy atmosphere. Incense is especially important for Zadkiel: choose a fragrance that might be used in a temple or church. Ask for divine protection as you set out on your spiritual journey.

Pre-record the visualisation on pages 52–3, or download it from www.workingwitharchangels.com, and follow the instructions for beginning your session. Here are the words to speak to Zadkiel (to be included in your recording):

Zadkiel, I acknowledge all the wonderful gifts in my life – the spiritual support from celestial realms, the love I receive from friends and family, the abundance of material comfort.

Remind me to give thanks on a daily basis, so that I do not forget how blessed I am.

Help me to bring abundance into the lives of those who are deprived in any way, so that they too can appreciate the blessings that are available to everyone.

Open my heart so that I can share with everyone, without judgement or restraint.

Advise me when I make decisions concerning money and other resources, so that I can give generously, but not become reckless.

If you have a symbolic gift for me to help me on my way, I am willing to receive it into my life.

Slowly come out of your meditation and record your experiences in your journal. Before blowing out the candle, recite the following invocation. Remember to send the light to someone who may need angelic help.

INVOCATION TO ZADKIEL

Zadkiel, archangel and comforter, hold my hand while I travel towards my goal. Give me all the things I need in order to move forwards. I know that you are infinitely generous – help me to receive the boundless abundance of life. Give me the confidence to open my heart and give freely to others.

Other ways to bring Zadkiel into your life

❖ Zadkiel's picture could be in the style of a Russian or Greek Orthodox icon. Choose rich colours and some gold, so that Zadkiel has a priestly air about him. You might be able to find a Christmas card with gold edging and use this as a frame for your icon.

❖ Give a party, asking all your friends to bring food. A 'pot-luck' party can magically demonstrate how, with a small contribution from everyone, a great feast will appear.

❖ One morning, perhaps at the weekend, lay your breakfast table with a tablecloth, special china and some flowers. Make a generous breakfast – and don't rush it. This will change the way you feel about your whole day. The world will feel abundant and generous!

❖ Go through your personal possessions, a bit at a time, acknowledging exactly how much you have. During this process look out for anything you could give away.

❖ Give a small treat to someone who is feeling hard up. Don't embarrass them by going over the top, but find something that will remind them that life's joys don't have to be expensive.

❖ Go to a religious service, particularly in a really beautiful temple, mosque, synagogue or church – somewhere you haven't been before. Don't be shy: most spiritual organisations welcome visitors – look them up in the phone book and call to find out the protocol.

❖ Make a list of all the available pleasures that cost nothing – libraries, museums, your local park and so on. Then spend a day experiencing how many good things come to you without opening your purse.

❖ Arrange a regular donation to a charity. Tithing is an ancient tradition and most modern teachers offering prosperity workshops suggest that giving 10 per cent of your income has a powerful effect on the amount that you receive yourself.

Zadkiel will help you understand that mercy is boundless, and that we don't need to be 'good' to receive universal bounty. Generosity of spirit is a powerful adjunct to love, which is why Raphael and Zadkiel together will help you move out of any feeling of material restriction.

Samael: the Tester

Also spelt: Sammael; may also be Satan

Contented limitation. Success.
I CHING

Sefira:	Severity
Keywords:	Discipline, adversity, limitations, lessons, responsibility, testing
Colours:	Snow white, silver
Gemstone:	Onyx
Flower remedy:	Rock rose
Essential oil:	Neroli
Planet:	Saturn

About Samael

Of all the archangels you will meet in this book, Samael may seem the most daunting. He comes as a counterbalance after the benevolence of Zadkiel, reminding us of our responsibilities.

Samael guards the *sefira* of Severity, sometimes translated as 'judgement', and his name means 'venom' or 'poison' of God. This may seem strange, but it presumably relates to the severe aspect of the Creator. Early kabbalistic writers recognised that severity is a necessary attribute in the divine Creation, which God can use to bring humans back into line.

Although traditional Kabbalah places Mars in Samael's position on the Tree, I associate severity with Saturn: in astrology, Saturn is the planetary god who provides limitations and, as 'the grim reaper', brings us to the final boundary of death.

Stories concerning Samael

When Moses made his mystical journey through the heavens, guided by Metatron, he met Samael in the seventh heaven. Samael was very different from the other angels Moses had encountered. From his crown to the soles of his feet he was covered in glaring eyes that Moses could not bear to look into; Metatron explained to Moses that Samael is the angel who takes away the human soul at death. Samael was about to descend to Earth to collect the soul of Job, and Moses prayed that he wouldn't have to meet Samael when his time came to die.

Samael is often included among the seven Archangels of the Presence, and he has an essential function on the Tree of Life as a counterbalance to human pride. It is surprising to read in some sources that Samael is the same spiritual being as Satan. However, in Hebrew the name *ha-satan* simply means the adversary, or tester. In early Jewish tradition there is no concept of fallen angels, and as far as the Tree of Life is concerned Samael is a heavenly being with a stern but necessary remit.

The Garden of Eden

The most famous story about human temptation is that of the Garden of Eden. In the biblical version of this myth the tester is a serpent, not a *satan*, but in a 1st-century text, *The Legend of Adam and Eve*, the serpent is said to be acting for Satan. Another legend, found in the *Aggadah*, tells us that Satan is the Archangel Samael.

According to the Book of Genesis, there were two trees growing in Eden, the Tree of Life and the Tree of Knowledge of Good and Evil (Genesis 2.9). God told the newly created Adam and Eve that they could eat anything in the garden except the fruit from the second tree (Genesis 2.17). Adam and Eve were innocent, like small children, and God, like a strict parent, set up a rule that would keep them that way. But if humans remain ignorant of good and evil they will never develop into responsible beings; discipline must arise from within, not be imposed from outside. Human beings have to break the rules in order to discover why the rules are there – Eve was tempted to eat the fruit and persuaded Adam to share it. After this God expelled them from Paradise to make their way in a world where they would grow up through encountering hardship, and also joy. Thus, Samael's temptation of Eve (and of ourselves) is actually a gift from God, a means to learn and grow.

The Testing of Job

In the story of Job, Job's tester is named Satan, and is described as one of the *bene elohim*, the Sons of God, with a rightful place in the heavenly court (Job 2.1). When God asks him where he has been, the archangel replies, 'From going to and fro on the earth'. God asks if Satan has considered his faithful servant Job, a man of great integrity who is never tempted to do evil. Satan points out that Job has an abundance of good things: if these were taken away he would curse God, not praise him.

God gives Satan permission to test Job – the only thing he is not permitted to do is to take away Job's life. Satan gets to work and Job has a terrible time: he is plagued with boils, and loses his wealth, his children and his home. But throughout his tribulations his love for God never wavers, and eventually he is rewarded with a super-abundance of wealth, many more children and his family gathered around him (Job 42.10).

During his trials the depressed Job talks to his friends, who discuss what he must have done to upset God. Then God himself speaks out of a whirlwind, pointing out to Job that a mere human being cannot understand all the mysteries of life: 'Where were you when I laid the foundations of the earth? Tell me if you have under-standing . . .' (Job 38.4–7).

Losses and pain that seem random and undeserved always present a problem for humans, who feel they should be able to understand the reasons for everything and resent it when unexpected difficul-ties arise – no wonder Samael has acquired a bad name. However, Archangel Samael (or the *satan*) can only create difficulties for humans with God's permission – he does not have a private agenda.

It is his task to test us in order to remind us of our human limitations, and these tests help us to mature and grow in wisdom.

Visions of Samael today

When I started my inner journeys to meet the archangels I was already very familiar with *I Ching*, the Book of Changes. In this oracle based on the ancient Chinese wisdom of the Tao, the constant interchange between the polarities of yin and yang is understood as essential to Creation. The hexagram 'Limitation' explains that although water itself is inexhaustible, a lake only holds a finite amount. Just as the lake needs boundaries in order to contain the water, in human life an individual becomes effective by setting limits and developing discrimination. Spiritual traditions throughout history have suggested that we should fast, or deny ourselves in other ways, in order to demonstrate our willingness to accept limitations.

MY VISION OF SAMAEL

My vision of Samael was exquisite – although chilly! I saw a stately woman, slender and very tall, wearing snowy white drapery that sparkled with crystals. Behind her the sky was the palest blue, radiating with white patterns that seemed to grow and stretch from her head and shoulders. When she moved her arms, these patterns glittered outwards from her fingers. She was making a constantly moving snowflake mandala. Her face was very clear-cut and regal, both serene and severe. She wore a crown of immense height that looked as though it was made of crystal carved with great precision into a three-storey palace with elaborate little turrets. This headdress added to her grandeur, and she also carried a fine sword like a fencer's rapier.

She moved slowly and gracefully, casting snowflake patterns around her, and her movements were accompanied by the sound of a bell – a gentle, almost muffled sound, on one note, as persistent as the ticking of a metronome. I felt she was stern, disciplined, focused – but not completely unfriendly. I got the impression that

---

> she wanted to help me achieve my highest potential, but I knew
> that would mean some difficult lessons.

My vision of Samael reminded me of Narnia,[51] the land ruled by the White Witch where it is always winter and never Christmas. Later in the story, after the child heroes have been severely tested, Father Christmas arrives and the lion Aslan heals the frozen land.

Many other classical allegories convey a similar message. For example, in John Bunyan's *Pilgrim's Progress*,[52] Christian has to suffer many trials on his way to the Celestial City, travelling through the Slough of Despond, imprisoned in Doubting Castle and tempted by Giant Despair – but always supported by a guide called Great-heart.

Samael's tests do not last for ever. They are processes that we need to go through and when they seem difficult we can remind ourselves that we are learning all the time. The board game Snakes and Ladders was originally based on the idea that we are climbing ladders to a spiritual state, while the tests (represented by snakes) of doubt and despair can make us slide down again. Then we have to start afresh, with a positive mind.

SAMAEL AND A DIFFICULT MARRIAGE

One of my students, Tamara, was initially very anxious about meeting Samael, but eventually this archangel became the most significant of all twelve of the angels, helping her through some really difficult issues. At the time when she worked with Samael, she was having some problems in her marriage.

Tamara told me that Samael had really surprised her. She received an inner message from the archangel, who told her not to be afraid, and asked her to accept help. After that she carried the Samael card from *The Angels' Script* around with her for four days. During that time she had some important insights about her marriage difficulties. At the same time she felt an inner support of strength and love, which helped her to become really clear about her options.

> Tamara realised that she could choose to leave her marriage, but that a more positive choice was to be clear with her husband and encourage him to work towards resolving their problems.

When things don't go as we wish it is tempting to return to childhood patterns, and many of us have a strong tendency to complain or find someone else to blame. Samael asks us to accept the fact that our personal behaviour plays a pivotal role in the way events and relationships unfold. We cannot change other people, nor should we try, but we have total freedom of choice over our own reactions and responses.

Calling on Samael

You may be thinking twice about meeting Archangel Samael, but there is nothing to fear from her. In fact, I am often surprised in my workshops that there are invariably a few people willing to work with her. This is either because they are going through a testing time that she could help them understand, or because they want to become more focused and disciplined and thus more effective.

Samael is not out to trick you, but is in fact a useful ally. If things seem tough, then an inner journey to meet Samael will provide insights into your difficulties. If you are unsure of your path or feeling a bit wobbly in your commitment to your goal, then Samael will help you get back on track, like a good life coach. Her stern lessons remind you that you create your life through your own actions; it is fruitless to complain or to blame others.

Ask yourself the following questions:

❖ Do you accept responsibility for all that has happened in your life?
❖ Have you imposed limitations on yourself that hinder your self-expression?
❖ Would you like to rearrange the structures in your life in order to fulfil your heart-felt desires?

Samael will help you address the fundamental issue of how you live your life, and how you spend your time in your present incarnation.

Your journey to meet Archangel Samael

In preparation for your journey, gather together items that will help you tune in to the disciplined, precise energy of Samael. Her colours are snow white, with maybe a touch of silver or stainless steel. Perhaps you could lay out your table in a distinct pattern, with geometric shapes: a series of small clear crystals would work well, radiating out from a white candle in the centre. Or you could decorate your table with cut-out paper snowflakes. (Take a piece of white paper, fold it several times, and then cut little triangles into each fold. When you unfold it you have a snowflake pattern.) Another option would be to use white or silver paper doilies, which have similar precise patterns. (Don't forget to keep the candle well away from the paper!)

Wear a talisman or crystal pendant that helps you feel clear and well focused. You might want to play solemn music to help you prepare to meet Samael, not with fear or anxiety in your heart, but with suitable gravity.

Pre-record the visualisation on pages 52–3, or download it from www.workingwitharchangels.com, and follow the instructions for beginning your session. Here are the words to speak to Samael (to be included in your recording):

Samael, help me to understand the lessons that I need to learn in this life.
Remind me to accept responsibility for everything I do and say.
Please bring into my mind any issues that I need to deal with consciously and strengthen me to address these with good grace.
Let me experience the true joy of life even in times of trouble and confusion, so that I do not fall into the trap of doubt and despair.
If you have a symbolic gift for me to help me on my way, I am willing to receive it into my life.

At the end of your meditation, before blowing out the candle, recite the following invocation, and send the light to someone who may need angelic help.

INVOCATION TO SAMAEL

Samael, archangel and tester, help me understand this testing time. Although your lessons can be painful, I realise that this is a learning process and that wisdom is gained through adversity. Encourage me to develop a sense of appropriate limitations, so that I can keep within the boundaries of my true path.

Other ways to bring Samael into your life

❖ Samael's icon can be created from anything white, especially if it is shiny or glittery, like snow. You could also cut folded paper to make snowflake patterns, and use them as a background, or for her gown.

❖ Create a timeline of your life on a large sheet of paper. Draw a straight line horizontally across it, halfway down. At the left-hand end of this line mark your birth date, and at the other end write the current date. Now divide the line into blocks of time, perhaps of five years each. Then sketch in all the key events in your life so far – going to school, graduating, marrying, divorcing, deaths of parents. Place these above or below the line according to their emotional significance. Failing an exam will go below the line, but not as far below as a divorce. If you got married the marker will (probably!) be above the line, but there might be another even more special event that goes way above that. After you have filled in all the major events, draw a connecting line between the points, noticing whether your life is generally a roller-coaster of extremes, or whether it has been difficult in patches, then up for a while, then more even.

❖ Use your timeline to consider the turning points when different choices would have significantly affected the outcome. Examine yourself for regrets. If you feel weighed down by 'if only I had done things differently', then work with Samael again, asking her to help you see the necessity of the lesson you had to learn.

❖ Make a list of activities you have been putting off that would make your life more efficient. Then set about achieving at least one, not with grim determination but with a light heart – do that pile of ironing while playing some great music!

❖ Offer to help someone who's having a tough time, encouraging them to see that it is a necessary process, and that perhaps when they look back later they will realise why they had to go through it.

❖ Consider what blocks you from succeeding: for example, you may want to sing in public, but feel too shy. Make a commitment to work towards shifting this limitation.

Samael is certainly a hard taskmaster, but her contribution to your life can be truly amazing. Without focus or discipline you can waste a great deal of time and energy. We all need structures and boundaries – but they should never be so rigid that they become immovable. Samael's snowflakes remind us that structures can be beautiful and light, melting away when they are no longer needed, and reforming for new situations.

The Holy Spirit

Breathe on me, breath of God,
Fill me with life anew,
That I may love what Thou dost love,
And do what Thou wouldst do
EDWIN HATCH

Non-sefira: Knowledge

The Holy Spirit marks the powerful place between the archangels on the lower and higher branches of the Tree of Life. You have now met all the archangels on the lower section, known as 'the creative builders', since they support Creation in a very tangible way. In our personal lives they can help us with our social interactions and in our spiritual development. The four archangels you are yet to meet dwell in the higher dimensions of the Tree and are hidden behind a veil, a cloud of unknowing which is the mysterious realm of the Holy Spirit.

The Holy Spirit has no attributes and we cannot begin to identify 'where' It exists. In Hebrew, Its name is *Ruah ha-Kodesh* meaning 'the breath', or 'the wind' of the Holy, and like the wind It is invisible – we only know Its power by Its effects. When we release ourselves from outer concerns and relax into the inner depths of our minds, we naturally open ourselves to the influence of the Holy Spirit. But we have to make an act of surrender in which we discard our ideas about how things should be, and allow the Holy Spirit to work through us. This process is much easier than we think – in fact, thinking gets in the way.

Most of the time our minds are in organising mode, in order to create outward effects: 'What do I need to buy for tea?' 'What's the quickest route to Newcastle?' 'I must phone the plumber!' and so on. These habitual mental activities are necessary for our survival in the world. The mind filters out any information unconnected with organising, and this filtering process invariably excludes the wisdom that naturally arises when the Holy Spirit is given the freedom to breathe through us.

The human mind is obsessed with time. We have inner clocks ticking constantly, measuring and calculating when things have to be done, and we are rarely 'present' in the moment. Being with the Holy Spirit is a timeless experience. While we are incarnated we can only catch glimpses of Its infinite realm, but people who go beyond their everyday selfhood and surrender to the Holy Spirit, if only briefly, have their lives transformed for ever. They describe being filled with knowledge, understanding the meaning of the universe and their essential role in Creation. This is not intellectual knowledge, but inner wisdom and the realisation of humanity's connection to the underlying unity of existence. With this 'knowledge' comes a sense of security and reassurance: that whatever is going on in the world, however random and chaotic it appears, actually has meaning.

The safest way to explore the mystery of the Holy Spirit is to meditate. Meditation is quite different from visualisation, or going on a guided journey. Visualisation is a way to access deep levels of our consciousness so that we can make contact with our Guardian Angel and the archangels. But it is still a mental process. Meditation is also a mental technique, but its goal is to still the mind, putting aside the intellect and so transcending thought and images.

When we go beyond thought we come to a still, silent space – the empty room of the Holy Spirit. It is a room with no floor, ceiling or walls. If we dive into this place we may, like a deep-sea diver, find pearls – of wisdom. The more often we dive, the more treasures we will bring back with us.

It isn't possible to create an image of the Holy Spirit, although sometimes it is depicted as a dove. When I created *The Angels' Script* cards, I asked my husband Will to design a symbolic picture representing the Holy Spirit as radiating light on a dark background. I thought It should look like the light at the end of the tunnel described by people who have had near-death experiences. One of my students, Annie, is a diver, and sometimes she goes on night dives. Here is her experience of working with this image.

When I focus on the Holy Spirit I have a sensation that is like being inside an underwater depth chamber, surrounded by metallic, tinny stillness. I do not find this unpleasant or frightening, but it does feel strange, very peaceful, something like infinity. I imagine that being in outer space must be very similar.

When I went on a night dive in Cornwall a large night-light was shining into the water from the dive boat, and as I came up from the bottom of the seabed this light became a large, white, shimmering circle surrounded by infinite cold darkness. However, instead of feeling uneasy about the dark water surrounding me as I usually do on night dives, I felt uplifted and started smiling and pointing upwards. I said inside my headset, 'Wow, that's just what it looks like!' – which surprised my dive buddy, who thought I was starting to suffer from lack of oxygen!

As I understand it, when we enter the quiet, still place of light and dark, we are suspending and surrendering our earthly being and relating to our inner being, which is then able to connect with a higher force or divine inspiration.

Meeting the Holy Spirit within you is a profound experience. It isn't possible for me to guide you to meet the Holy Spirit in this book, and even in workshops I can only suggest ways to allow this experience to happen. Regularly using the meditation technique suggested in Appendix 1, pages 227–8, will encourage it to arise naturally, without effort, and when the time is right for you.

Summary 3: Zadkiel, Samael and the Holy Spirit

Together Archangels Zadkiel and Samael help us to develop as rounded human beings, who understand how expansion and generosity can be sensibly balanced by restraint and self-discipline. They teach us to be responsible grown-ups, capable of wise social interactions. Then the Holy Spirit awaits us, whenever we are ready to turn to Its boundless knowledge.

Archangel Zadkiel teaches mercy and inclusiveness. We all need to be able to give freely and extend our boundaries to embrace the whole universe. Zadkiel encourages us like a favourite grandfather, giving us sweeties for every success. His benevolence is wide-ranging and unlimited, so he will help you understand how amazing it is to open your heart to all Creation, without prejudice or judgement. Zadkiel brings wealth and abundance, teaching us that what we give out comes back to us, so that our cup is constantly overflowing.

Archangel Samael counterbalances Zadkiel's expansive energy by teaching us discernment and the usefulness of structures and boundaries. She is our stern parent, pushing us to make effective use of our gifts, reminding us of our duties and responsibilities – not only to others but also to ourselves. When Samael tests us, we discover exactly how strong we are – like steel that is tempered in fire, we become stronger with every new challenge. Samael does not rule out humour: a sense of fun helps us to overcome adverse circumstances. Her severity is essential for spiritual growth.

The Holy Spirit is ever-present, and in times of crisis people often have a spiritual encounter that wakens them to Its presence. In a gentler way, when we meditate we can sink into the still, quiet space within and discover this arena of divine simplicity. It is like entering an empty room, a place of all possibilities, in which we can work from a clean slate. True knowledge is the realisation that what appears to be fixed material reality is underpinned by a spiritual energy that cannot be measured or contained.

In the next four chapters you will be meeting the archangels who work beyond 'the veil' in the highest realms of being: Raziel, Zaphkiel, Metatron and the Shekinah offer insights that go beyond our personal lives. They are concerned with humanity as a whole, supporting us collectively as we evolve towards a higher state of consciousness.

Raziel: the Keeper of the Mysteries

Also called Gallizur

. . . here is my secret, a very simple secret: it is only with the heart that one can see rightly; what is essential is invisible to the eye.

ANTOINE DE SAINT-EXUPERY

Sefira:	Wisdom
Keywords:	Revelation, wisdom, insight, clarity, awakening
Colours:	Electric blue
Gemstone:	Topaz
Flower remedy:	Vervain
Essential oil:	Peppermint
Planet:	Uranus

About Raziel

Raziel's name means 'secret' or 'mystery' of God, and his *sefira* is Wisdom. For the ancients, wisdom meant not just good sense, but also knowledge of the 'mysteries'. God sends Raziel to help humanity by teaching us the hidden mysteries of Creation, which today would include physics and cosmology. He has no traditional connection with a planet, but I associate this archangel with Uranus. Astrologically, Uranus represents the ability to receive sudden insights, especially into esoteric matters, which is in keeping with the ancient legends about Raziel.

Raziel's other name, Gallizur, means 'he who reveals the secrets of the Rock' – the 'Rock' being God himself. In the *Aggadah*, Raziel stands behind the curtains concealing the Divine Throne, where he hears and sees everything that God is designing for humanity's destiny. Then, on God's command, he reveals God's teachings and plans to the prophets. When Raziel stands before the Throne he keeps his wings outstretched, so that the fire of the seraphim will not scorch passing angels. Moses trembled when he caught a glimpse of Raziel as he travelled through the heavens, but God helped him to pass by unhurt.

Stories concerning Raziel

The most famous story about Raziel, also from the *Aggadah*, concerns the book of secrets that he gave to Adam. After being expelled from Paradise with Eve, Adam prays for God's forgiveness and asks the angels for 'knowledge and understanding'. After three days of constant prayer, Raziel appears to him with a book, saying he has been sent to answer Adam's petitions. Raziel tells Adam that he can become wise through the contents of this sacred book, which will tell him the future and how to prepare for disasters ahead, and will also provide human beings with medical knowledge on how to use herbs to cure disease. The book will enable humans to know when there will be famines, plagues or wars – it is in fact a survival hand- book for the human race. Adam is told that it must be handed to his descendants, who must read it with a devout heart and humble mind and obey its precepts.

When Raziel read from this holy book, Adam fell down, trem- bling with fear. But the archangel said: 'Arise and be of good courage. Be not afraid. Take the book from me and keep it, for thou wilt draw knowledge from it thyself and become wise, and thou will teach its contents to all those who shall be found worthy of knowing what it contains . . . only wise and God-fearing people who are secure against wicked counsels.'

The legend goes on to tell us how the jealous angels, resenting the wisdom given to human beings, stole the Book of Raziel and threw it into the sea. Adam searched for it in vain, and fasted and prayed until God called in Rahab, the Angel of the Sea, to return it to him. When Adam died the book was hidden in a cavern, and later the prophet Enoch was led to its hiding place in a dream. Enoch drew all his knowledge of nature, of the Earth and of the heavens from this book, and became even wiser than Adam. Once he had committed all this wisdom to memory, Enoch hid the book again.

When God decided to create the Flood he wanted Noah to have the wisdom in the Book of Raziel and this time sent Raphael to restore it to human hands. It contained the instructions for building the ark, written on tablets of sapphire (it was clearly a magical book), which Noah enclosed in a gold casket. The Book of Raziel also served as a timepiece while Noah and his family were in the ark, allowing them to calculate the passage of time. When Noah died he entrusted it to his son Shem and it was then handed down through the generations to Abraham, Jacob, Levi, Moses, Joshua and King Solomon – who learned all his wisdom from it, including mastery over demons.

In the 13th century some kabbalists claimed to possess material from Raziel's book and the tradition of its existence continued into the 18th century. In 1701 a printed version of an old manuscript, called *Ha-Sefer Raziel* ('The Book of Raziel'), full of cosmological and astrological wisdom, was published in Amsterdam. A copy is still kept in a hermetic library in Amsterdam.

The 'wisdom' in Raziel's book of information is esoteric – it gives Adam insight into the hidden workings of the universe. It is also practical and scientific, containing cosmology and medical knowledge. In astrology all these topics are associated with the planet Uranus, which brings new understanding to inventors, researchers, scientists and philosophers. Anyone who has ever had a 'Eureka!' moment, when they suddenly understood something, will know how Raziel communicates with human beings. Understanding how the universe works has always been a human goal, and knowledge brings responsibility. When we discovered how to split the atom we were faced with the possibility of the total extinction of our species. If this kind of information was in Raziel's book, no wonder the archangel said that it should only be passed on to people who are 'secure against wicked counsels'.

Visions of Raziel today

MY VISION OF RAZIEL

When I met Raziel I saw a very fine, cobweb-like structure made of tiny filaments of light – like fibre optics, only even more delicate. These fibres seemed to hum and tinkle, vibrating at very high speed. I felt that each one might be making a different sound or saying a different word, if only I was on the right wavelength to hear them. Then I saw the faint outline and form of a face that was at once very young and ancient. It was a serene face but it had intensity about it, a slight sharpness that removed it from being totally peaceful. The archangel's head was swathed in pale blue lights, folding and turning, while the fibres parted to make a radiant halo which continued to vibrate and flicker. His eyes were a startling blue and seemed to be full of wisdom. As I looked into them I could see stars and galaxies stretching into an infinite distance. He was brilliant and I was amazed.

A Welsh student of mine, Caitlin, was in her late forties when she started one of my postal courses. During the month when she was working closely with Raziel, a highly unexpected event set the whole family in turmoil.

RAZIEL, ARCHANGEL OF THE UNEXPECTED

When Caitlin was a young teenager, her brother Thomas (five years her senior) got into trouble with the police for a fairly minor offence. His family and his solicitor tried to reassure him that he would probably just be put on probation, but Thomas was terrified of going to prison. It was also clear that he felt dreadfully ashamed and couldn't look his parents in the eyes. On the morning his case was to be heard, Thomas went missing. He had emptied a savings account and a local bus driver had seen him get off at the train station. It seemed likely that he had gone to London, but no amount of research or appeals provided any clue as to his whereabouts.

Twenty-five years later, Caitlin was working with Raziel and wondering what surprises the archangel might bring into her life, when her mother phoned in a very emotional state, saying she had received a call from Thomas who wanted to be reconciled with his family. He told his mother that he had originally gone to Scotland, worked in bars and cafés under a false name, then worked his passage on a ship to New Zealand to start a fresh life.

When Thomas and his family were eventually reunited, there was a mixture of emotions – some of the family were naturally still angry, but mostly he was welcomed like a prodigal son and everyone gathered for a party. Caitlin encouraged him to get legal advice so that the issue of dodging his court appearance would be laid to rest. Everyone involved had to turn their thoughts around – including Thomas, who discovered that his legal situation was not nearly as bad as he had believed all those years ago.

Calling on Raziel

Raziel helps you to see through problems and think 'out of the box'. He brings exciting new possibilities into your life and opens channels to higher wisdom. His sudden awakening of your inner wisdom can be startling and often promotes a series of dramatic adjustments in your life. At first the result may seem chaotic, but you will realise that this is a necessary part of the process of your mental realignment. Raziel encourages total freedom of thought and brings inspirations from the highest source. Before meeting him, ask yourself the following questions:

❖ Are you open to surprise?
❖ Can you see the creativity in chaos?
❖ Are you looking forward to rapid change?
❖ Are you willing to seem eccentric and go against the acceptable way to do things?

Notice how often people say they want to change for the better, when in reality they fear change and want everything to stay the same. When working with Raziel, be prepared for a radical shift in your perspective.

A journey to meet Archangel Raziel

For your Raziel table, find electric-blue fabric or shiny wrapping paper with holographic patterns. A silver-blue candle would be appropriate, or instead of a candle you might be able to find a glitter ball to spread patterns of light around your room, or a fibre-optic lamp giving out fine strands of neon that change colours.

Bring together anything that catches your eye during the days leading up to your date with this archangel. Don't try to be rational about your choice, but use your intuition to pick up all kinds of odd things. You may have played the party game where players have to remember a group of disparate objects laid out on a tray. Imagine you are collecting items for a game like this, which may have no obvious connection.

Pre-record the visualisation on pages 52–3, or download it from www.workingwithangels.com, and follow the instructions for beginning your session. Here are the words to speak to Raziel (to be included in your recording):

Raziel, help me to see new solutions to old problems in my life, so that I can build a new and exciting vision for my life.

Encourage me to let go of old habits that do not serve me, and open my eyes to the new possibilities that occur whenever I experience a crisis.

Expand my understanding and wisdom, so that I realise the under-lying processes in human life that are drawing us all towards a higher state of consciousness.

Allow me to accept changes in my life and in the world without fear and anxiety, so that I welcome the dramatic shifts that are necessary for human evolution.

If you have a symbolic gift for me to help me on my way, I am willing to receive it into my life.

When you have come out of your meditation in the usual way (see pages 50–1), recite the following invocation to Raziel. Send light to all those who need it before blowing out your candle.

INVOCATION TO RAZIEL

Raziel, Archangel of Divine Mysteries, like a father you provide me with insight so that I may become an independent and responsible person. Illuminate my path for me, so that I may clearly see the way forwards. Allow me to know the truth with the deepest part of my mind, so that I can carry the light with me wherever I go.

Other ways to bring Raziel into your life

❖ Make your archangel icon from any materials to hand – for Raziel you might use some shiny sweet wrappers or kitchen foil. Keep your Raziel reminder somewhere unusual – near the kitchen sink or on your bathroom cupboard. He is the master of surprises, so give him the opportunity to surprise you and your visitors.

❖ Look at the objects you collected for your table and see if you can work out why they called to you. Each item will have a message of some kind even if it looks initially to be quite ordinary.

❖ Look at the items again, and see if you can make any connections between them – even if the connections seem quite outlandish and strange.

❖ Think about your present life and your everyday routines. Imagine an event that would bring sudden change. While I was writing this book a tornado hit a London street and several sturdy Victorian houses had to be demolished. This is a negative example of sudden change – but you could imagine a positive one. For example, an elderly aunt leaves you thousands of pounds, but only on condition that you leave your home in a quiet English market town and move to Africa. How would you handle a change like this?

❖ Read about scientists who have changed the way we live, such as Marie Curie, who discovered radium, Alexander Fleming, who developed penicillin, or Copernicus, who revolutionised the way Europeans thought about the solar system.

❖ Learn how to use a dowsing pendulum. This will allow you to gain insights into all kinds of hidden knowledge, such as discovering which herbs or supplements can improve your health.

❖ Get your birth chart drawn up by an astrologer, and also ask for a chart for the present year (called a 'solar return'), so that you gain some insights into the possibilities for your immediate future.[53]

All the archangels are very powerful beings, but the archangels at the top of the Tree of Life are supercharged! You can think of Raziel as a higher vibration of Gabriel: Gabriel communicates with words, pictures and music, while Raziel brings sudden insights. Gabriel brings changes which you can see unfolding if you are observant, while Raziel's changes are unexpected and dramatic. It is easier to resist Gabriel – you can have a dialogue with him – but resistance is useless with Raziel because the change is upon you before you are aware it has even started. Remember, however, that even the most startling changes have been brought into your life because a deep part of you requires a fundamental shift to happen in order for you to develop as a whole person. They say that discovery favours the prepared mind: if you are prepared to accept dramatic change for your spiritual growth, then the powerful insights you need will come to you.

Zaphkiel: the Compassionate Mother

Possibly the same archangel as Zophiel, Iofiel or Jophiel

Across the gateway of my heart
I wrote 'No thoroughfare',
But love came laughing by, and cried
'I enter everywhere.'
HERBERT SHIPMAN

Sefira:	Understanding
Keywords:	Unconditional love, compassion, peace, freedom, grace
Colours:	Rose pink
Gemstone:	Ligure
Flower remedy:	Clematis
Essential oil:	Rose
Planet:	Neptune

About Zaphkiel

Zaphkiel stands at the gate of light called 'Understanding'. She is on the feminine side of the Tree of Life and in the occult tradition she is called 'the Mother' (while Raziel on the masculine side is called 'the Father'). One of her titles is 'Angel of Contemplation'. Her name means 'knowledge of God', and she is said to be in charge of the cherubim, who are filled with divine knowledge because they are able to see all four corners of the universe, and rule over all four elements.

I associate Zaphkiel with the planet Neptune who rules the ocean, which is boundless like the unconditional motherly love of Zaphkiel. The 16th-century occultist Agrippa allocates an archangel to each of the prophets, or patriarchs, and says that Zaphkiel worked with Noah, who saved the future of humanity and other living creatures from the great Flood with his ark.

Stories concerning Zaphkiel

There are hardly any traditional stories about Zaphkiel, perhaps because her motherly energy is more generalised than that of other angels, and because she works behind the scenes. She does not arrive in a grand style, or deliver the secrets of the universe – but in her own quiet way she sustains us as we wrestle with life's daily problems.

Zaphkiel may be the same archangel as Zophiel, who is also said to work with the cherubim. Zophiel's name means 'God's spy', which seems apt for an archangel who goes about her business unnoticed. The name Zophiel itself is sometimes spelt Jophiel or Iofiel, when it means 'beauty of God', and that name is also very suitable for the motherly Zaphkiel. By contrast, as Zophiel, this archangel accompanies Michael into battle. There are always many layers of meaning behind the names of archangels, and we cannot hope to put them into neat little boxes.

Every spiritual tradition has a 'Divine Mother' figure offering unconditional love to all humanity. The oriental goddess of compassion, Kuan Yin, is one example. For the ancient Egyptians the goddess Isis, with her son Osiris, was a mother figure. In Christianity she is Mary, the mother of Jesus of Nazareth. One of Mary's titles is *stella maris* – the star of the sea – and Zaphkiel represents a higher vibration of Auriel, the motherly archangel who rules the Moon, which has such a powerful effect on the ocean.

Think how water can quietly seep into every crack and crevice – this is what spiritual love can do when we accept it. The work of Mother Teresa of Calcutta was inspired by this love; she was connected to the Divine Mother in her spirit and worked unceasingly for those who were neglected and ignored. In this way, she became an earthly manifestation of heavenly love, which has no limitations – Shakespeare describes it beautifully in *Romeo and Juliet*:

My bounty is as boundless as the sea
My love as deep; the more I give to thee
The more I have, for both are infinite.

Visions of Zaphkiel today

MY VISION OF ZAPHKIEL

When I asked to meet Zaphkiel I found myself standing by a calm ocean, stretching as far as I could see. The water was rippling with tiny waves, trimmed with white foam. The sky above was a soft blue and the water was a transparent blue-green. I stood on the sand with my feet on the very edge of the sea, which gently bathed my toes. The sound of the water swished and chuckled, and there seemed to be a very faint breeze. I felt very peaceful and my consciousness expanded into the calm air and the water, so that I felt totally united with the elements around me. I felt a great sense of delight and stretched my arms out and upwards. As I did so I noticed what seemed to be small creatures rising from the sea, as though imitating me. But the creatures were flowers, pink rosebuds that opened up into blossoms as they emerged.

One of the roses stretched up and up and its petals expanded into the sky until I could hardly see any blue. I could hear faint voices, like a choir singing a Gregorian chant. Then the centre of the big rose became a woman's face with a blissful smile and a halo of pink light, and the petals became wings encircling her face – dainty wings with finely etched feathers. The sky behind her twinkled with gold and silver stars that sent spinning rays of light into all the spaces which were not filled with her own rosy aura. I have no idea how long I spent in a state of bliss before I came back to my everyday self.

Many of my students are healers and they find it very easy to make a strong connection to Raphael. I often receive enrolment forms from people who are already doing some kind of healing – spiritual healing or Reiki for example – and they mention having experienced the presence of Raphael while giving healing. I explain that the Archangel Zaphkiel carries a similar vibration, functioning at a deeper level, beyond the personal. Several healers have found that they can work with Raphael to help people with everyday issues, especially when they arise out of currently poor relationships, but that Zaphkiel can also help clients whose discomfort, physical or psychological, is rooted in something older – perhaps a family issue that goes back generations.

ZAPHKIEL AND THE MISSING MOTHER

Claire is an experienced Reiki healer. One of her clients, a middle-aged bachelor called Peter, came to her with severe skin problems that had plagued him since adolescence, Peter had tried conventional ointments, herbal remedies, homeopathy and even hypnotherapy, but even when he found some short-term relief, the problem kept returning.

On his first visit Claire decided to give Peter the usual Reiki healing, but also to ask for angelic help. She had been reading about Zaphkiel in her course material and specifically asked to work with her. As she worked, Claire experienced a soft pink light surrounding herself and Peter, who was lying on the couch. She felt a loving presence and received an inner prompt suggesting that she should ask Peter about his family background, especially on his mother's side.

Peter told her that he had been brought up by his aunt because his mother had disappeared when he was only three months old. No one knew what had happened to her and Claire gently suggested that the constantly weeping skin was a sign that he was still crying for his mother. Peter burst into tears and sobbed for a long time. He said that his aunt had been very stern with him and had always told him that he shouldn't care about a woman who hadn't cared for him. So Peter had never had permission to grieve over his missing mother.

Peter came back for more Reiki treatments and Claire always asked Zaphkiel to support his healing. During that time Peter had a dream in which a shadowy female figure spoke to him, telling him that he was loved.

A few months later Peter's skin had improved considerably and he decided to start going to a singles club, feeling that he was now ready to meet someone.

Calling on Zaphkiel

In order to benefit from a loving relationship with Zaphkiel, we have to set aside our everyday wants and needs and function from a deeper state of being, one in which we can sacrifice self-interest and personal desire. Our ego is a necessary structure that allows us to function in the world, but we also have the potential to function from our souls and to open our hearts, allowing divine blessings to flow through us into the world.

You can think of your ego as a gatekeeper, living in one of those lodges that guard the entrance to a grand mansion. The gatekeeper's job is to keep an eye on the everyday requirements of the estate. However, there is a risk of becoming a little self-important, forgetting that the owner of the big house is the one who ultimately provides the wealth. The owner, who might be a royal personage like a princess, is your soul – that spark of the Divine within you which is the source of all the goodness and love in your life. Zaphkiel teaches you that Divine blessings are limitless and that your gatekeeper needs to relax and accept abundant love, and to share it unconditionally.

Before meeting Zaphkiel, ask yourself:

❖ Do you feel connected to the boundless love of the Divine Mother?
❖ Are you able to open your heart to the whole world, without conditions?
❖ Can you imagine your love reaching out into the cosmos?
❖ Do you know for certain that your own soul has no beginning and no end?

Working with Zaphkiel will help you release old blocks and barriers to loving, not simply at a personal, intimate level, but to experiencing the mystical love that encompasses all Creation – both light and dark.

Your journey to meet Archangel Zaphkiel

In preparation for your session, delicate pink fabrics, white lace, chiffon or veiling would make the perfect table cover for Zaphkiel, along with a vase of roses or a sprinkling of dried rose petals scattered over it. Introduce any images that bring to mind divine motherhood – perhaps a small statue of Kuan Yin or Mother Mary. You may be able to find an angel carved from pale pink rose quartz in a shop selling crystals. Use rose-scented incense or aromatherapy spray. There is a wonderful album of sacred music sung by women, called *Feather on the Breath of God*, with music composed by the 11th-century Abbess Hildegarde of Bingen. You could find this music quite uplifting as a preparation to meet Zaphkiel. Lastly, include lots of white feathers on your table.

You may know the painting *The Light of the World*, which depicts Jesus with a lamp in his hand standing by an ivy-covered door. It was painted by the Victorian artist Holman Hunt. When someone suggested to him that the picture was unfinished because there was no handle on the door, Hunt replied: 'This is the door to the human heart and it can only be opened from the inside.' Similarly, the Christian mystic Dame Julian of Norwich wrote that God is like sunshine and it is only because we keep our shutters closed that we live in darkness. Zaphkiel is the archangel who will help you open your shutters, and unlock the door to your heart.

Pre-record the visualisation on pages 52–3, or download it from www.workingwitharchangels.com, and follow the instructions for beginning your session. Here are the words to speak to Zaphkiel (to be included in your recording):

> *Zaphkiel, help me dismantle all the barriers that prevent me from receiving and giving unconditional love.*
> *Allow me to hold a vision of beauty and truth in my heart, even when life seems difficult.*
> *Let me see the divine spark in everyone, however negative they may appear to be.*
> *Remind me of the endless, magical power of love that sustains us all.*
> *If you have a symbolic gift for me to help me on my way, I am willing to receive it into my life.*

When you come out of your meditation, after writing in your journal, remind yourself that Zaphkiel is present in your life by saying the following invocation aloud. Then send the light from your candle with a blessing to all Creation.

INVOCATION TO ZAPHKIEL

Zaphkiel, Archangel of Divine Compassion, like a mother you cradle me. Encourage me to open my heart without fear, catch me when I stumble on my path. Allow me to creep back to your arms when I feel weak. I know I am not measured and unconditional love is always available to me. Help me to give, even as I receive.

Other ways to bring Zaphkiel into your life

❖ Create an image that reminds you of Zaphkiel's gentle, loving energy. Your icon does not have to be a masterpiece, just a symbolic image that brings the archangels into your everyday surroundings.

❖ Make a list of anything you can remember doing that still makes you feel guilty. Sit quietly and allow the loving power of Zaphkiel to fill your heart and wash away the old guilt. You may need to do this more than once. When you feel you are truly blessed, the following tasks will be more effective.

❖ Every day for a week send silent blessings to every living creature or plant that comes to your attention as you go about your daily life.

❖ Look at the things in your life that you enjoy and send blessings to the people who made or supplied them – workers you will never meet.

❖ Make a list of people who make you feel uncomfortable for whatever reason. Light a candle and sit quietly with your list. Visualise each person in turn and imagine yourself in their presence, giving them your blessing.

❖ Think of the difficulties that people can undergo, and consider which kind of stress or pain makes the most impression on you – is it the plight of small children, orphaned by war? Or homeless people on city streets? Whatever strikes the deepest chord, visualise those people and send blessings to them. Then make a generous contribution to an appropriate charity.

❖ Now choose a group of people in trouble who make you feel angry because you think they should be able to sort themselves out, or that their problems are their own fault – drug addicts, teenage gangs, beggars, etc. Meditate and send them your unconditional blessings, and then find a practical way to help some of them – either financially or by giving your time.

❖ Make a gift just for fun to someone who may not be needy or deserving – and give it anonymously.

❖ Finally, just so that you don't start feeling too holy, treat yourself to something special – chocolates, champagne, flowers, whatever! You can share your treat if you want, but you could just enjoy it on your own.

Zaphkiel's motto is 'all you need is love'. This divine love goes beyond personal feelings and romance: it is about giving and not counting the cost; it is about surrendering our own immediate requirements for something greater in order to experience the boundless possibilities of our divine inheritance.

Metatron: the Presence

Also spelt: Metratton, Metaraon;
another name for Metatron is Jofiel,
also spelt Jophiel

*The birds, on fire with love, said 'How can the moth
save itself from the flame, when it wishes to be one with
the light?'*
FARID AL DINN ATTAR

Sefira:	Crown
Keywords:	Judgement, choice, karma, commitment, obligation
Colours:	Bright white light
Gemstone:	Diamond
Flower remedy:	Mimulus
Essential oil:	Sandalwood
Planet	Pluto

About Metatron

Metatron sits at the top of the Tree of Life, at the *sefira* called the Crown, and he has the most awe-inspiring reputation of all the archangels. The meaning of his name has never been satisfactorily explained: some scholars suggest that it comes from the Latin verb *metator*, 'to measure'; another suggestion is that it means 'great throne' (*meta tron*). One description of Metatron, which would fit either of these meanings, tells us that he sits on a heavenly throne from which he can mete out reward and punishment, like God himself. The idea of 'measuring' is reminiscent of the Egyptian god Anubis, who weighed the souls of the dead at the final judgement.

I associate Metatron with the planet Pluto, who in astrology brings dramatic transformation into our lives. Pluto was the Roman god of the Underworld; his Greek name was Hades, from a Greek word meaning 'unseen'. His glory was such that humans would die if they saw him. Metatron's radiance is similarly overwhelming.

Metatron resides at the top of the Tree of Life, while his twin brother Sandalphon oversees the base of the Tree, the Kingdom, which is rooted in the material world. In the Talmud, Metatron is the link between the human and the Divine and is charged with the sustenance of humanity.

Stories concerning Metatron

Like Sandalphon, Metatron was once a human being, the prophet Enoch who lived before the time of Noah's Flood. The Book of Genesis describes how Enoch vanished from the Earth, because God 'took him' (Genesis 5.24); in other words, Enoch did not die an ordinary death, but was taken straight to heaven.[54] Many centuries later Rabbi Ishmael described in the *Sefer Hekhalot* ('The Book of the Divine Palaces')[55] how he made a mystical journey to the seventh heaven where Metatron supported his desire to have a vision of the Throne of Glory. (Humans were not necessarily welcome in heaven!) In this story Metatron tells Ishmael how he was transformed into an angel:

> . . . *the Holy One took me to the Throne of Glory . . . my flesh turned to flame, my sinews to blazing fire, my bones to juniper coals, my eyelashes to lightning flashes, my eyeballs to fiery torches, the hairs on my head to flame, my limbs to wings of burning fire . . . and earthquakes roared all around me.*

After this complete transformation Metatron was given a throne to sit on, with ministering angels beside him. God gave him a crown engraved with the holy letters YHVH (Yawheh), which stand for the name of God himself, indicating that God had elevated the prophet to the highest possible divine status. Metatron is sometimes called 'the lesser YHVH'. He was clothed in light and granted superhuman qualities, including the ability to speak the languages of humans and animals, and to assign gifts of greatness, royalty and honour to earthly princes.

Metatron tells Ishmael how an earlier visitor to heaven, a seeker called Aher, seeing him seated on his throne, thought there must be two Gods in heaven – since according to Jewish tradition angels, having no limbs, cannot sit down. When God heard Aher voicing his amazement, he quickly made it clear who was the real boss – Metatron was severely punished and told never to sit down again.

This story makes it quite clear that, however grand an angel might appear, there is only one God. Even so, Metatron retained his majestic status. He has been called King of the Angels, Prince of the Divine Presence, Chancellor of Heaven, Chief of all the Ministering Angels, and Angel of the Covenant. Like God himself he has 72 names, one of which is Jofiel (sometimes spelt Jophiel), which means 'beauty of God'. The name Jophiel is sometimes included in lists of the seven angels who 'stand before the throne'.

Another title for Metatron is the 'Liberating Angel', the angel who releases us from our human trials at the point of death or during any transformative spiritual experience. Metatron allows us to shed our illusion of separateness and release our old karmic bonds, enabling us to surrender to the divine power and become one with the Divine.

Metatron is considered to be mightier than Archangel Michael, although one Jewish text claims that Metatron is the same archangel as Michael. Both Michael and Metatron have been described as 'the heavenly scribe'. Metatron is credited with writing Psalm 37, which advises us to 'be still before the Lord and wait patiently', and also prophesies that the meek will inherit the Earth, reminding us that all human deeds will eventually have to be justified.

Visions of Metatron today

I have read several accounts by people who have had near-death experiences describing how, before they returned to their bodies, they came into the presence of a light-form that asked them to review their life so far. This being demands honesty but is also loving, with no sense of anger or punishment. It has never been named, but it seems very possible that it is the Archangel Metatron, who has been said to perform a similar role when people die, not judging them but giving them the opportunity of judging themselves.

Shortly before going on my inner journey to meet Metatron, I had a dream in which I found myself in a beautiful garden full of wonderful plants and flowers, like an Arabian paradise. Through the garden ran a glittering stream and on the near side hovered all the archangels I had met so far. Beyond the stream I could see Metatron as a brilliant white flame of light topped with a golden crown which sparkled with coloured jewels. I stood on my side of the stream, willing the archangel to come over, but he stayed where he was. I wanted to cross over, but the stream was too wide. When I woke I wondered whether I would have the same kind of problem when I asked to meet Metatron in meditation, but later I realised that the dream had been a preparation for our meeting.

MY VISION OF METATRON

When I asked to meet Metatron I felt energy collecting around the crown of my head. Then I saw a brilliant white-gold globe of light. I couldn't see any facial features, but I felt I was being watched. The globe radiated beams that seemed to expand into infinity. Shining rays of red and gold pushed upwards like a fountain, creating a huge semi-circle of flames or feathers.

There was a tremendous rushing noise and a beating sound, like a bass drum, which became louder and louder. As the drumming increased in volume the brilliant feathers created a vast shower of tiny lights, rather like an extravagant firework display. Each light seemed to be humming a different note, creating an overall harmony of sound. The drumming continued to grow louder until it suddenly stopped. The silence was deafening by contrast; everything became very still and gradually the colours diminished until nothing was left but a brilliant white light. I sat in the stillness and the light and felt a great sense of calm and completion.

Metatron's power may be felt as a presence, and when you meet him you may not hear any words. A few years ago Mary-Anne, a London-based nurse in her early forties, wrote to me describing an experience that was quite awe-inspiring.

MARCHING TO A DIFFERENT DRUM

One morning when I was still half asleep, I felt semi-paralysed by a presence that can only be described as powerful and wise. At first I was afraid and felt very threatened by this presence. I seemed to be in a waking dream and I called out several times for protection from Archangel Michael.

The presence continued to move through me. It felt like the vibration of a very loud drum. The name Metatron came into my mind. After calling out his name I felt the pressure lift and I woke up properly. The memory of the experience remained vivid for the next 24 hours. I am still not clear what it all meant, but I know that Metatron is now working with me – time will tell where the journey with Metatron will lead me.

Spiritual development often brings up very intense experiences that cannot be rationalised at the time. While writing this chapter I called Mary-Anne to ask whether she now had a greater understanding of her vision. She told me that at the time she had been at a major turning point in her life and that Metatron had been prompting her to change her career. The same experience had happened to her on more than one occasion since she wrote her first account. Each time she felt quite unsettled and almost fearful, feeling she was being pushed into making a major decision – one from which she wanted to hold back. She became aware that the intensity came from somewhere very deep inside her, and that it was a signal for change.

I was interested in the drumming sound, particularly as I had heard it myself. It reminded me of the expression 'to march to a different drum', used to describe people who seem to run their lives according to an inner directive, rather than conform to the usual social values. I also thought of the metronome, an instrument for keeping time, and felt that perhaps Metatron is our inner conductor, reminding us to listen to our own inner drummer and march accordingly.

Calling on Metatron

You may feel nervous about meeting this amazingly powerful archangel; his reputation as a judge can make him seem quite threatening. But if you have done your work with Zaphkiel, who reassures us that we are loved unconditionally, you will be prepared at a soul level to discuss any leftover karmic issues with the King of the Archangels. Talking to Metatron gives you an opportunity to read the story of your life so far, observe any errors and re-evaluate how you are living. He helps you to look at your life with great clarity, not judging you, but enabling you to judge your own actions against the criteria you would like to live by.

If you do want to go on an inner journey to meet Metatron, I suggest you give yourself extra time before and after this process. As you may have gathered, such a meeting can be quite mind-blowing. Generally speaking, all the archangels will only give you what you can handle – but even that might be more than you expect. So if you want to work seriously with Metatron, it would be a good idea to plan a quiet weekend for your session, with plenty of wholesome food, time to go walking in nature and someone to talk to afterwards about your experience.

Before your session, ask yourself the following questions:

❖ Do you accept that where you are in your life now is a natural result of your own thoughts and actions?
❖ Are there any old karmic bonds that you still need to release?
❖ Are you prepared to redress any mistakes wherever possible?
❖ Are you willing to move forwards into a life based on integrity and clarity of purpose?

Metatron's throne-room is the fundamental power-house of Creation, and in personal terms this means that if you have clarity and integrity you will be able to develop your life effectively.

A journey to meet Archangel Metatron

Simplicity is the key to this process. For your preparation, a plain white cloth, perhaps a quartz crystal and a white candle on your table are quite sufficient. For this meeting, also put out a brand-new notebook together with a black pen. On the cover write 'Book of Life'. You are going to ask Metatron to show you the book of your life, and afterwards you will be writing a record of the interview. This is extremely important: what you write down will be a point of reference for you in the future.

Pre-record the visualisation on pages 52–3, or download it from www.workingwitharchangels.com, and follow the instructions for beginning your session. Here are the words to speak to Metatron (to be included in your recording):

*Metatron, I come before your throne in humility, being aware that
    unconditional love is available to all of us.*
*Show me the book of my life and point out anything that I need to
    work with to make reparation for my mistakes.*
Leave a two-minute pause on your tape.
*Help me to make wise choices, based on integrity of purpose, and be
    at my side constantly, reminding me that I am the creative power
    in my own life.*
*If you have a symbolic gift for me to help me on my way, I am
    willing to receive it into my life.*

After opening your eyes, write an account of this interview in the notebook you prepared for this task. Date the account for future reference.

Complete your session by speaking the following invocation:

> **INVOCATION TO METATRON**
>
> Metatron, all-powerful judge, I have dedicated myself to a path of transformation and bring my actions into the bright light of your all-seeing eye. I have walked through the darkness and have surrendered all my hopes and desires, seeking to act only in accordance with divine will. Draw me in to the centre and source of all being, that I may be renewed.

Finally, send the light from your candle with a blessing to all Creation.

Other ways to bring Metatron into your life

❖ Your icon for Metatron could be a crown: you could easily use gold paper or card to make the kind of crown you find in Christmas crackers. Design it to fit your head. Edge it with white feathers, then add a few sparkling jewels – when I worked on theatre costumes we used fruit gums for rubies and emeralds. Remind yourself of your sovereignty over your own life by looking in the mirror wearing the crown.

❖ Consider how often you make excuses for your behaviour, explaining to yourself or others that your choices are based on outside pressures beyond your control. Take time to write some of these in your special notebook, and ask yourself whether it is really true that other influences oblige you to behave in certain ways.

❖ Write out the following affirmation:
I AM THE CREATIVE POWER IN MY OWN LIFE.
Make several copies and pin them up around your home. Make a small copy the size of a credit card to keep in your wallet.

❖ Every day, as soon as you wake up, stand up straight and say the affirmation out loud at least three times before getting your early-morning cup of tea or coffee:
I AM THE CREATIVE POWER IN MY OWN LIFE.

❖ Find a small object, like a crystal or talisman, which reminds you of your power of choice. Keep this with you wherever you go,

and when you are in a state of self-doubt touch it, and repeat the affirmation again, silently if necessary:
I AM THE CREATIVE POWER IN MY OWN LIFE.

❖ Continue to use your notebook for any observations that arise in your mind about how you do things, the choices you make and any reasons you give yourself for sometimes acting without integrity.

Metatron's essential quality is power. You may feel that your personal arena of power is very small, but the power you have is actually enormous. Most of us abdicate using our capacity to make wise choices, partly due to laziness, partly due to fear of the consequences. But even under dire circumstances you can take power over your own life – as demonstrated by Nelson Mandela, who spent 27 years in prison. Mahatma Gandhi refused to allow threats to his life to override his choice to walk among people without bodyguards. He was prepared to die to uphold his commitment to peaceful solutions to conflict. Being aware of our own divinity means that no government or dictator can exert power over us: our souls are always free and never die.

Collectively we have the power to improve life for our fellow humans, to eradicate poverty, illness and war. Starting in our own circle of influence we can begin to shift human consciousness into a higher gear. Real power does not lie in using tanks and missiles to resolve problems, because aggression only escalates fear and leads to further problems. Divine power resides in the hearts and minds of individuals, and when we change our way of thinking and being, we will create heaven on Earth.

The Shekinah: the Queen of Heaven

Other names: the Matrona, Rachel

One day she will be with us
in all her glory.
A flash of pure gold
merging with deep azure
will herald her coming.
She will carry in her hand a perfect crystal,
she will be accompanied
by the quiet ones in silent attendance.
ANNE M. HILL

Sefira:	The Crown
Keywords:	Mercy, karmic release, wholeness, blessings
Colours:	Night-sky blue
Gemstone:	Agate
Flower remedy:	Water violet
Essential oil:	Chamomile
Heavenly Body:	Charon, the moon of Pluto

About the Shekinah

The Shekinah is the unseen presence of the Divine in Creation; her name comes from the Hebrew verb *shachan*, 'to reside'[56] (indicating that she is residing in Creation, even though we may not be aware of her). As the Queen of Heaven, at the Crown *sefira* with Metatron, she is also the greatest feminine power in Creation. In some kabbalistic texts she appears at the foot of the Tree of Life, in the Kingdom. One of her other names is the Matrona, indicating that she is a mother figure and Metatron's bride. In the *Aggadah* we are told that the Shekinah hovers over marriage beds and blesses the union with her presence. In the Kabbalah she is sometimes called Rachel, which means 'ewe', a name suggestive of her capacity for gentle surrender.

Charon, the Shekinah's celestial body, relates to Pluto just as our Moon relates to planet Earth, both circling around a single centre. These heavenly bodies provide a symbolic manifestation of the relationships between the Shekinah and Metatron, and of Auriel and Sandalphon. In the same way that Sandalphon is twin brother to Metatron, we can think of the Shekinah as twin sister to Auriel.

The *Zohar* dedicates a huge portion of its teachings to the Shekinah, who is included in a section about the nature of the godhead rather than the section about angels, where Metatron appears. However, the *Zohar* does mention her as an angel that appeared to Moses, Jacob and Moses's brother Aaron, who received the kiss of death from her. The *Zohar* tells us that the Shekinah has no light of her own and no definite colour, but that she acts as a mirror for all nuances of colour and the rays of light and shadows they create – in this way she contains all the variations of the created world. She is likened to a lily and a rose because these flowers change as they unfold.

Stories concerning the Shekinah

According to the Talmud, when Adam and Eve were expelled from Paradise the Shekinah hid herself from human eyes. She remained behind, enthroned above a cherub on the Tree of Life in the Garden of Eden, her splendour being 65,000 times brighter than the Sun. Nevertheless, although she is hidden from humanity, the *Zohar* confirms that she is still present, sustaining the world as its great mother, like a foundation stone placed at the centre of the world:

When the Holy One created the world, He threw down a precious stone from beneath His throne of glory and it sank into the deep . . .

> *One edge of the stone became lodged in the deeps and the other in the realms above. There was another edge, a single point – the Shekinah – which is in the middle of the world and the world expanded from there, to the right and to the left, and upon all sides, and it is sustained from this central point.*[57]

From this stone the world receives its flow of blessings. In Hebrew the ever flow of divine blessings is called *shefa*, and people who pray and meditate are contributing to the flow of blessings that can then be distributed throughout the world.

The Tree of Life is based on a symmetrical pattern in which the top and bottom are reflections of each other: you cannot have a crown without a kingdom, or vice versa. This is why so many paradoxes surround the Shekinah: she is both at the top of the Tree of Life and hidden yet present at the foot of the Tree; she is described as shadowy, yet radiating splendour and light much greater than the Sun. In kabbalistic tradition, when humanity has sorted out its problems and recognised its own divinity we will live in peace and the Shekinah will reside in glory at the foot of the Tree of Life. Meanwhile, we could say that Auriel is her representative in the Kingdom.

Visions of the Shekinah today

MY VISION OF THE SHEKINAH

When I asked to meet the Shekinah I found myself before a door made of crystals. The facets were like mirrors and I could see many reflections of my own face. As I kept gazing, the multitude of Theolyns gradually melted into a single image of a face that was like mine, but not quite. I had the impression that I was being shown a deeper layer of my own being. I remembered how, as a teenager, I had often looked into a mirror, gazing into my own eyes, wondering if I could discover something about my own soul. Then I inwardly heard the words from St Paul's Epistle to the Corinthians: 'For now we see through a glass darkly, but then face to face: now I know in part, but then I shall know even as also I am known . . .' (1 Corinthians 13.12).

These words seemed to be coming from part of my own mind, as though the mirror image had prompted them. I felt I was still only in touch with the surface; I wanted to go through the mirror and touch the invisible world on the other side, where I thought the Shekinah must be dwelling. Part of me was pushing against what seemed to be the barrier of the reflections.

Suddenly I was able to let go of my intellect and my desire to push against the boundary and I found myself surrounded by an energy that wrapped me up in loving softness. Everything became dark and I heard a woman's voice saying, 'The source of all life is love, which is stronger than death . . . set me as seal upon thine heart.'

And I saw a face in the shadows and caught a glimpse of a mysterious smile. I thought perhaps the face was the same one I had seen in the mirror.

Later I realised that the words spoken by the mysterious woman also had a biblical connection; they are similar to a verse in the Song of Solomon which begins: 'Set me as a seal upon thine heart, as a seal upon thine arm: for love is strong as death . . .' (Song of Solomon 8.6). The Song of Solomon is a mystical hymn to divine love, likening the divine source to a lover. The next verse tells us: 'Many waters cannot quench love, neither can the floods drown it . . .'

Because I had no religion in my family background I have never been a great reader of the Bible, but as I child of eight I discovered the Song of Solomon in a poetry book. Looking back I realise that the mystical beauty of its words had a profound effect on me – I believe it was the beginning of my spiritual journey. The poetry book was *The Golden Treasury of English and American Verse*,[58] and my father, who was never present in my life, had given it to my mother. To have access to that 'treasury' at such an early age was a priceless gift.

The effect of meeting the Shekinah was very blissful. I went around for several days with a smile on my face, and since then I have always felt that I can let go of all my anxieties and allow myself to relax into the quiet energy of the Shekinah. I think of her as a hammock in which I can rest, supported by divine love. And I regularly remind myself of the phrase 'set me as a seal upon your heart', which for me means to be constantly aware of the strength of love to conquer all things.

THE LADY OF THE MOUNTAIN

The poem quoted at the start of this chapter is from 'The Lady of the Mountain' by Anne Hill, a member of a Welsh meditation group called the Order of Sancta Sophia. Over 20 years ago, while meditating at an evening service in Pennal church, Anne heard the words: 'Ask, ask who is the Lady of the Mountain . . . the fire . . . the ancient wisdom.'

She talked to the rector, Geraint ap Iowerth, about her experience. He had been thinking of disbanding the meditation group, but the message that came through Anne prompted a new flowering. A small space over the rectory garage was converted into a chapel dedicated to Hagia Sofia – the holy wisdom.[59]

Over the last 20 years Anne has developed an inner relationship with a feminine presence who calls herself 'the Lady', who on one occasion commanded her: 'Come draw me out, the world has need of me.'

It was this command that prompted her to share her poems and meditations in her self-published book. In one of her poems 'the Lady' says that she is everywhere:

in the clamouring sounds of the city,
in the silence of the lake,
in the breaking of ocean waves . . .
in every living creature,
in every tree, every plant, every flower.

The above words, and many of the messages in the meditations, as well as the idea that 'the Lady' would carry a 'perfect crystal', makes me think that this feminine presence is the Shekinah. It seems to me that the feminine aspect of divine power will inevitably have different names according to different cultures. Sophia (or Sofia) is a Greek name used in the Christian tradition, especially in the Orthodox Church. In Hinduism, the feminine face of the masculine god Shiva is called the Shakti. Wherever we live, whatever our personal spiritual heritage, 'the Lady' can speak to us, using a language or images that we can understand. The message 'the world has need of me' seems to be a very powerful indication of our collective need to bring the feminine back into Western culture, which has been dominated for so long by left-brained thinking and the masculine urge towards achievement and conquest.

Calling on the Shekinah

The Shekinah is always present for all of us. Making conscious contact with her is a powerful experience that can change the way you understand life. When people first meet their Guardian Angel they realise that they will never be alone again. But who supports your Guardian Angel? Yes, it is the Shekinah. Your Guardian Angel is a very personal guide and support, but the Shekinah goes beyond the personal. Like Metatron, she has been called the Liberating Angel because she demonstrates that our sense of separation and aloneness is an illusion. We live in a shadowland in which it is difficult to see the Divine at work, but when we work with the Shekinah during quiet retreat and prayer, we access the timeless, hidden place where she resides and can feel gathered back into her comfort and strength.

Before meeting the Shekinah, ask yourself:

❖ Can I see the beauty of the Divine in all Creation?
❖ Can I love all living creatures, including people, whatever their qualities and behaviour?
❖ Can I accept all events as part of my process towards understanding and deeper love?

These are deep challenges. We are trained from birth to view the world as divided into good and evil. Meeting the Shekinah is like dipping into an ancient well whose source is the boundless ocean of divine love where there are no divisions, and we need to be willing to surrender our preconceptions and our social programming before she can fill us with her love.

A journey to meet the Shekinah

Preparations for meeting the Shekinah can be very simple indeed. I suggest you keep your table minimal, with just a single white candle and few additions such as a crystal – if you want to use one, choose a piece of clear quartz. Wrap yourself in something special – perhaps a shawl or a fine soft blanket, preferably one you can drape over your head to give you the feeling of being cloaked or hidden.

Pre-record the visualisation on pages 52–3, or download it from www.workingwitharchangels.com, and follow the instructions for beginning your session. Here are the words to speak to the Shekinah (to be included in your recording):

Dearly beloved Shekinah, shift the narrow thoughts in my mind that block my ability to experience your love.
Untie the knots in my heart that inhibit my ability to give love.
Open the windows of my soul and allow the sunshine of divine love to fill my whole being and liberate me from the illusion of separation.
If you have a symbolic gift for me to help me on my way, I am willing to receive it into my life.

At the end of your meditation and before blowing out the candle, recite the following invocation, sending the light to someone who may need angelic help.

INVOCATION TO THE SHEKINAH

Shekinah, Queen of Heaven, I come to your door seeking to be reconnected with the source of all life. I know I am a child of the Divine and that all things that seem painful and dark are part of the shadowland I live in for the time being. Guide me towards wholeness that I may come out of the shadows into the light.

Other ways to bring the Shekinah into your life

❖ For her icon the Shekinah, like Metatron, needs a crown. Hers could be dark blue, studded with silver stars, but create whatever seems right to you. If you ask, she will guide you.

❖ Book yourself a retreat – one where there is a very simple timetable. Commit to taking regular retreats during the year.

❖ Read the mystical poetry of Rumi, the 13th-century Persian poet, or the Song of Solomon.

❖ Listen to classical or other relaxation music that helps you transcend your everyday thoughts, allowing you to experience the sense of being supported by divine love.

❖ Spend time watching the world. What is the view from your window? Allow yourself to see its glory, whether it includes cars and buses and busy people, or trees and plants. Give yourself plenty of time for this 'open-eyed meditation', so that you can start seeing the world through new eyes. It may take a while and some practice, but eventually you will have a breakthrough – an experience of being connected to everything. Then your heart will overflow with love.

The Shekinah is the source of all blessings. Ask her to watch over you when you sleep. Acknowledge her presence in the world every morning as soon as you rise.

Summary 4: Raziel, Zaphkiel, Metatron and the Shekinah

All four archangels at the top of the Tree of Life present powerful energy fields that can assist us collectively as we strive for spiritual evolution. When we work with any of these magnificent beings, we connect to the deepest reaches of divinity, the very foundation of human consciousness, and we are likely to provoke intense and potent changes in the way we experience life.

Archangel Raziel opens the door to new thinking. He is revolutionary, overturning the old in order to allow new possibilities. Raziel offers unusual solutions to problems, whether physical, emotional, mental or spiritual. By ordinary social standards Raziel's approach is eccentric – in order to find an answer to a question or a problem that defies your usual methods, you have to think in a completely different way. For the ancients his *sefira*, Wisdom, did not simply mean spiritual maturity but, rather, insight into the hidden mechanics of the universe. Raziel is able to crack open the thought boxes that lock us into our limited beliefs. Then we have a sudden realisation, the light pours in: Eureka! I've got it!

Archangel Zaphkiel is our compassionate mother, a constant nurturing presence who opens our hearts to the boundless love of the Divine. Accepting her spiritual nourishment strengthens us and allows us to give unconditional love and blessings. Her *sefira*, Understanding, offers the ability to empathise with all creatures. Working with Zaphkiel encourages our psychic gifts and enables us to receive and transmit blessings and messages of love and healing.

Archangel Metatron is the great judge who requires us to live by rigorous standards of integrity and respect – both for ourselves and for our fellow creatures. His message is that everything matters. However small or insignificant some event or social exchange may seem to be, it creates a mark in the Book of Life and a karmic resonance in your personal history and in the annals of humanity. Metatron can help you take up your spiritual crown – with his help you will understand your purpose so that you can live a properly focused, satisfying life.

The Shekinah cloaks herself in mystery and calls us to go deeper into our spirituality, so that eventually we will meet her face to face. Surrender is the key to her magic. When we stop trying with our minds or hoping with our hearts, she steps into the space we have forgotten – the vast, immeasurable region of our soul. Her crown is invisible, but glorious. Working with the archangels in the upper reaches of the Tree will transform your life in ways you cannot imagine. Be prepared for the unexpected, the magical and the miraculous.

Completion: Keeping in Touch with the Archangels of the Tree of Life

Now you have met twelve powerful helpers, and have been introduced to the possibilities offered by the Holy Spirit – so make the most of your new alliances. You can now communicate with any of these archangels at any time, according to your needs.

Whenever something happens to you that presents a challenge, whether it is a career or health issue, a relationship problem or a general feeling that you are not getting what you want out of life, think about these magnificent archangels. Decide which one could help make you feel more confident and face these issues, not just with equanimity, but with total confidence. You can either work with one archangel, or use the invocation to the archangels given in Part 2, Chapter 1 (p. 46).

Here is an additional visualisation for bedtime, which will keep you connected to the archangels. It is a very beautiful Tree of Life exercise to do as you to go sleep.

THE HAMMOCK
❖ When you are lying in bed at night, preferably flat on your back, imagine you are aligned with the Tree of Life, with Sandalphon and Auriel at your feet, and Metatron and the Shekinah at your crown.

❖ Visualise the other archangels at the gates of light as pinpoints, like Christmas tree lights, and the golden threads running between them as strings that make up a hammock beneath you.

❖ Now allow your whole body to sink into the hammock, which supports you in a cradle of light. Breathe deeply and let yourself go . . . Sleep sweetly.

In Part 3 you will be meeting twelve more archangels – the Guardian Angels of the twelve signs of the zodiac. As you will discover, they can also support your life at an inner level, and can team up with your Guardian Angel and the Tree of Life archangels to create an unstoppable 'dream team' who can be on your case whenever you ask.

PART 3

The Archangels of the Zodiac

How to work with the Zodiac Archangels

Each zodiac sign has an archangel as its guardian. Everyone born under a particular sign will naturally be protected and guided by its archangel – for example, everyone born under the Sun sign of Taurus is in the soul group guided by Ashmodiel. The other heavenly bodies – the Moon, Mercury, Venus, Mars and so on – also move through the same signs and will be influenced by the archangels as well. Thus, if you were born with the Moon in the sign of Taurus, then Ashmodiel would be a strong helper for you, even if your Sun sign is not Taurus.

You could consult an astrologer or look on an Internet site to find out about the placement of the Moon or the planets on your birth date, though this isn't essential. You can ask any of the zodiac archangels for help, even if they don't govern your Sun sign, and even if you have no other information about your birth chart.

You may know that the twelve signs are grouped into four elements, fire, air, water, earth, which are related to the Four Worlds. The signs are also grouped into three qualities – cardinal, fixed and mutable. The quality tells us how the element functions in Creation:

❖ Cardinal signs: people who work as initiators, beginning projects, pushing new concepts forward, e.g. the author of a book.
❖ Fixed signs: people who make the project happen, e.g. the publisher and printer.
❖ Mutable signs: people who take the finished product out into the world, e.g. the distributor and sales team.

The diagram below shows which element, quality and world relates to each archangel, and will help you decide which archangel you may want to work with after you have met the archangel of your own sign.

I recommend that everyone should start by having a conversation with the archangel of their own Sun sign, and then move on to meet all the others. After meeting your own zodiac archangel you could then meet the archangel for the sign opposite your own. For example, if you were born under the sign of Aries, Saraquael is your archangel. After meeting Saraquael, go to meet Zuriel, archangel for Libra, on the opposite side of the zodiac. Talking to your opposite archangel is a very helpful process, because it gives you a mirror. The diagram will help you identify your opposite archangel, and shows you all the names of the archangels, with their signs.

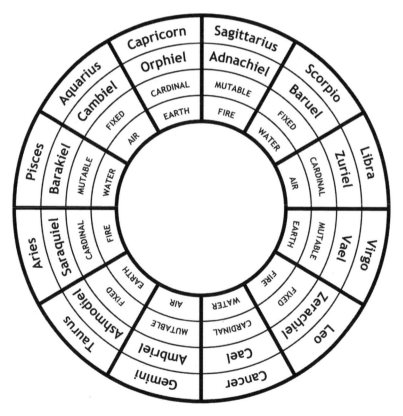

The archangels of the zodiac

Another approach is to work around the zodiac, meeting each archangel in turn. This process will help you understand other people, their needs and drives, and why we are all so different. Learning to allow others to be who they are, even when very different from yourself, will enormously improve your interactions with others. The archangels show us that every individual is a unique thread in the divine tapestry of Creation without whom the world would be diminished.

You could also try working with the archangels of one element at a time. If you are feeling low in spirits and looking for a boost of energy, try calling on all three fire archangels. If you need grounding, call on all the earth archangels.

Meeting one of the Zodiac Archangels

Use the visualisation below to meet any of the zodiac archangels – the one who rules your Sun sign, the one who rules your Moon sign, or any other archangel who could help you develop particular qualities or deal with specific issues.

Before your journey, record the words below and insert the requests that are listed in the section for the archangel you have chosen. The twelve zodiac archangel visualistations are also available on www.workingwitharchangels.com.

❖ Ask your Guardian Angel to come with you on a journey to meet the zodiac archangel you have chosen. Feel your Guardian Angel's presence beside you.

❖ Imagine you are in huge, circular room. The walls around you are shining gold and set with crystals and precious stones.

❖ As you stand in the middle of this magical room, you can hear beautiful music, as though choirs of angels are singing. Around the edges of the room you can see twelve different doors, each encrusted with different-coloured jewels, and each with a name engraved on it in beautiful calligraphy.

❖ You can see the name of the archangel you want to work with and you notice that the door is gently swinging open. Beyond

the door is a room full of light that seems to welcome you. You
have the sensation of being drawn towards the light without
any effort.

❖ The zodiac archangel meets you at the door, radiating wonderful
colours that wrap themselves around you.

❖ Now you can ask the archangel for guidance and for help with
any specific questions.

❖ **At this point add the words given in the section for your
chosen archangel.**

❖ **Leave at least two minutes' silence on your tape to allow for
a conversation to take place when you meet the archangel.**

❖ Ask the archangel if he or she has a symbolic gift that will help
you.

❖ Thank the archangel for his or her help and any gift you have
been given, then say goodbye.

❖ You move effortlessly back into the golden room and watch the
archangel's door slide gently back into place.

❖ Ask your guardian angel to take you back to your everyday world.

❖ Before opening your eyes do some stretches, wriggle your hands
and feet, and breathe deeply.

❖ Open your eyes slowly and write down your experience in your
journal.

Now it is time to meet the zodiac archangels.

SARAQUAEL

Archangel for the sign of ARIES
21 March – 20 April

ELEMENT Fire (yang)

PLANETARY ARCHANGEL
Hanael (Mars)

SACRED STONES Diamond,
bloodstone

SACRED GIFT A diamond crown

QUALITY Initiating

KEYWORDS Hope, action,
creativity, clarity

COLOUR Red

METAL Iron

MANIFESTATION Enterprise,
energy

ABOUT SARAQUAEL

Saraquael is not only an archangel, but also a six-winged seraph, blazing with fire. The element of fire clears away the old and initiates the new. Saraquael encourages us to be bold and take risks, in order to push forwards.

Many innovative thinkers and inventors were born under the sign of Aries, with Saraquael as their guiding archangel. Leonardo da Vinci is a famous example – his ideas were years ahead of those of other inventors. Isambard Kingdom Brunel is a favourite of mine: he was probably the world's greatest engineer and a giant figure of the Industrial Revolution. Saraquael not only gives us access to higher realms where we can access brilliant ideas, but also provides the energy to keep going. Leonardo was a multi-talented creator and Brunel had enormous stamina and mental focus.

Saraquael's energy is unconventional – as though he is saying that there is no fixed way to do something, so why not experiment? People born with Archangel Saraquael over-lighting their lives are creative and inventive, and always seeking challenges. They are able to initiate far-reaching concepts that will inspire others. They often seem to have access to an endless source of energy. If they develop spiritual integrity, they can become shining lights in the wider society.

HOW SARAQUAEL CAN HELP YOU

Saraquael works with Hanael, the Archangel for the planet Mars, to provide a direct connection to the infinite power-house of the Divine, and can help you to develop your full potential. Saraquael can help anyone develop creativity. His energy is very childlike, encouraging innovation and helping us to 'think out of the box'. You can ask Saraquael for help if you are:

❖ looking for new, creative ideas,
❖ seeking a solution to a problem,
❖ faced with a personal challenge, whether physical or emotional,
❖ feeling low in spirits, lacking in energy, or unfocused,
❖ recovering from a debilitating illness.

MEETING SARAQUAEL

Download the visualisation from www.workingwitharchangels.com, or pre-record and follow the instructions for the visualisation on pages 52–3, including the following words to speak to Saraquael:

Archangel Saraquael, remind me of my true purpose and help me direct my energy towards my divine potential.
Be present in my life whenever I am feeling stuck or downhearted. Urge me on whenever I feel like giving up.
Bring new possibilities into my life so that I can develop my unique talents.
Clear my mind of any prejudice or judgement that gets in the way of my creative possibilities.
Help me to meet life's challenges with clarity and spiritual integrity.

IDEAS FOR CONNECTING TO SARAQUAEL'S ENERGY

❖ Join a class that challenges you and asks you to think differently.
❖ Cut out words and phrases from magazines or newspapers and re-arrange them to create a poem.
❖ Listen to a well-known song and think of new words to the same tune.
❖ Obtain some children's wooden blocks and build a tower – then

knock it down and start again. Enjoy both taking it down and thinking of new ways to rebuild it.

❖ Experiment with listening to music you think you won't like. Allow your mind to be clear of prejudice and see what happens.

Choose a challenge for the coming week, another for the coming month and another for the year. Be really clear what your goal is. Ask Saraquael to support your focus and provide the energy you need.

ASHMODIEL

Archangel for the sign of TAURUS
21 April – 20 May

ELEMENT Earth (yin)

PLANETARY ARCHANGEL Sandalphon
(Earth)

SACRED STONES Emerald,
moss agate

SACRED GIFT An emerald necklace

QUALITY Fixed

KEYWORDS Peace, stability

COLOUR Green

METAL Copper

MANIFESTATION
Steadfastness, stewardship

ABOUT ASHMODIEL

Ashmodiel brings the invisible glory of our dreams and hopes into physical reality. She is determined to create heaven on Earth because she understands that visions have no value until they are made real and tangible. Her solid, practical commitment supports the unfolding process of nature – the mountains, valleys, lakes, deserts, volcanoes and glaciers of our planet are all in Ashmodiel's domain. She can be gentle, but she can also be stern when we do not honour nature, and is saddened by the recent natural disasters caused by humanity's lack of respect for nature.

One of the most beautiful manifestations of nature is the human body, and people who work with Ashmodiel are often concerned with the body, either as performers – through dance like Darcey Bussell, or in the field of medical care like Florence Nightingale. Ashmodiel supports the development of all artistic skills as these allow us to express our inner dreams, manifesting them in the world as paintings, music, theatre and films.

People who have Ashmodiel as their Sun sign archangel are able to make lasting impressions in the physical world; they are practical creators who can bring ideas into concrete form in the physical world. They often have the ability to attract great wealth and abundance, and make good business people. Ashmodiel helps us to improve everyday life, and encourages us to manage financial affairs efficiently.

HOW ASHMODIEL CAN HELP YOU

Ashmodiel works with Sandalphon, the Archangel for Planet Earth, and can help you manifest your inspirations and dreams in the world. You can ask Ashmodiel for help if you:

- ❖ are beginning a new project that requires practical application, such as setting up a new home, putting on a theatrical production or starting a business,
- ❖ want to improve your physical health through a discipline such as yoga, dance or gymnastics,
- ❖ need to re-evaluate your lifestyle so that you can make the best use of your resources and attract what you need.

MEETING ASHMODIEL

Download the visualisation from www.workingwitharchangels.com, or pre-record and follow the instructions for the visualisation on pages 52–3, including the following words to speak to Ashmodiel:

Archangel Ashmodiel, fill me with determination and serene power so that I can work towards my goals with calm conviction.

Bring me the resources I need in order to manifest my vision for the benefit of all.

Help me become a wise protector and steward of nature, using natural resources to create beauty and harmony.

Guide me in the practical affairs of my life and help me use money and other gifts wisely.

IDEAS FOR CONNECTING TO ASHMODIEL'S ENERGY

- ❖ Make a list of your unfulfilled dreams, choose one and write down the resources or skills you will need to realise it. Create a wall chart with a visual image representing the goal, and list the practical steps needed to make it happen. Start acting on these.
- ❖ Choose a practical or physical skill that you would like to acquire, whether it is knitting, gardening, skating, dancing, painting or something else. Sign up for a class, or get a good book or DVD on the subject. Get started.

❖ Explore exchanging your skills and talents with like-minded people, or organise a group with a practical goal that will benefit the community.

Ashmodiel has a calm, serene and competent energy that is very comforting. She is a builder and will help you carry through your plans, giving you complete conviction that you will be able achieve your goals.

AMBRIEL

Archangel for the sign of GEMINI
21 May – 20 June

ELEMENT Air (yang)

PLANETARY ARCHANGEL Gabriel
(Mercury)

SACRED STONES Beryl, aquamarine

SACRED GIFT A horn of agate

QUALITY Mutable

KEYWORDS Variety, joy

COLOUR Yellow

METAL Quicksilver

MANIFESTATION Invention,
change

ABOUT AMBRIEL

All angels move lightly and quickly, but Ambriel moves at top speed, whispering in the trees, skimming the clouds, dipping and curving into the depths of the Earth. He moves easily through all the worlds, from light to dark and back again, bringing divine inspiration to humanity. Music and poetry are excellent vehicles for Ambriel's quicksilver energy. Paul McCartney and William Butler Yeats are good examples.

Ambriel is a shape-shifter, constantly seeking to express divine truths in ways that are not bound by old rules. The songwriter Bob Dylan has always been connected to the magic of Ambriel, able to pull inspirational songs from the ether and also change his style in order to surprise his listeners. Actors often work with this energy – Johnny Depp is a good example – as do stand-up comedians such as Joan Rivers, famous for her fast talking.

Brilliance of mind and problem-solving abilities are also on Ambriel's menu: Sir Arthur Conan Doyle, creator of Sherlock Holmes, was born under Ambriel's sign. So was John Nash, the mathematician with the 'beautiful mind', whose life story was recently portrayed in the film of that name. Nash had such an intense connection with this sparkling mental energy that he found it difficult to live in a normal social context. His struggle to cope with his own genius reminds us that we all need to balance our lives so that our mental processes are in harmony with our physical and emotional needs.

HOW AMBRIEL CAN HELP YOU

Ambriel works with Gabriel, Archangel for Mercury, helping you to adapt to change, and to actively look for divine guidance and inspiration. He helps people to see both sides whenever there is a conflict of interest. Ask Ambriel for help if you:

❖ are learning a new language, or studying for an exam, especially one involving problem-solving, such as mathematics,
❖ want to learn to play a musical instrument,
❖ are required to give a talk and feel nervous about public speaking,
❖ want to write something inspiring – a song, a prayer, a meditation or a poem,
❖ want to act as a channel for higher dimensions,[60]
❖ want to facilitate understanding where people are in conflict.

MEETING AMBRIEL

Download the visualisation from www.workingwitharchangels.com, or pre-record and follow the instructions for the visualisation on pages 52–3, including the following words to speak to Ambriel:

Archangel Ambriel, open my mind to the sacred words of the Divine and the music of the spheres.
Bring me celestial visions and help me communicate with integrity and wisdom.
Allow me to see through problems and find solutions that bring benefits to everyone.
Help me act as an inspiration to others, facilitating understanding and communication.

IDEAS FOR CONNECTING TO AMBRIEL'S ENERGY

❖ Develop problem-solving skills by doing regular mathematical, crossword or Sudoku puzzles.
❖ Learn to play chess.

❖ Learn to play a musical instrument.

❖ Offer to talk to a local group about a favourite subject of yours – *without* using any notes.

❖ Join a local drama group and practise acting the part of someone unlike yourself; or join a class in stand-up comedy or performance poetry.

❖ Meditate and ask for messages from angels for yourself and for people you know. Keep a pen nearby to write down anything that is given to you.

❖ Ambriel will bring you messages from the Divine but he asks you to communicate with integrity and commitment to the truth.

CAEL

Archangel for the sign of CANCER
22 June – 22 July

ELEMENT Water (yin)

PLANETARY ARCHANGEL Auriel (Moon)

SACRED STONES Pearl, selenite

SACRED GIFT A mother-of-pearl breastplate

QUALITY Cardinal (initiating)

KEYWORDS Patience, sympathy

COLOUR Sea blue

METAL Silver

MANIFESTATION Imagination, nurture

ABOUT CAEL

Archangel Cael has a nurturing, feminine energy. She is connected to the wellspring of divine love; like a cascading waterfall or a running brook she brings joy and delight. You can feel her shimmering energy on moonlit nights, and the fairies are under her care.

Cael welcomes those in need of tender loving care and calls small children to her knees. She is a wise teacher and a prophetess, offering her oracle of intuitive wisdom, drawn from the depths of the cosmic ocean, to anyone who will listen.

Your family will benefit from the loving care of Cael, who can help you access ancestral wisdom, especially from the maternal line. Because her soft, motherly energy tends to act behind the scenes, people who work with it do not often step into the limelight. However, one very famous person of recent times was born under Cael's sign – Princess Diana, whose concern for all children and desire to be a good mother are legendary.

HOW CAEL CAN HELP YOU

Cael works with Auriel, the Archangel of the Moon; she can help you whenever you are in need of tender loving care, or when you find yourself caring for others. You can ask Cael for help if you:

- want to improve your family relationships or heal ancestral wounds,
- want to send love and support to children who are away from home,
- are organising a family event, such as a wedding or a baby blessing,
- would like to look after babies, stray kittens, new-born chicks or any other young creatures,
- are a healer or in a caring profession, or have to take on a caring role for an elderly or disabled relative.

MEETING CAEL

Download the visualisation from www.workingwitharchangels.com, or pre-record and follow the instructions for the visualisation on pages 52–3, including the following words to speak to Cael:

Archangel Cael, open my heart to your tender loving care so that it fills every corner of my being.
Allow me to receive love and comfort from my family and other people around me.
Help me develop my intuition so that I can understand the needs of others and empathise with them at a deep level.
Guide me to situations where I can nurture anyone in need, young or old.

IDEAS FOR CONNECTING TO CAEL'S ENERGY

- Pin your favourite pictures of children on a noticeboard, even if they are not of your own children. Every time you pass the board send them a blessing.
- Offer to help a local organisation providing care for children, pets or disabled people.
- If you have no children in your family, sponsor children in Third World countries.
- Write a thank-you letter to anyone who supported and encouraged you as a child. If they are still alive send it to them; if they have left your life, for whatever reason, burn the letter and ask the angels to deliver the message.
- If you feel let down by someone who could have given you loving support, allow yourself to cry about this. Write down your feelings.

Light a candle, and ask Cael to come into your heart and repair the sadness.

❖ If you haven't seen your family for a while, find an excuse for a gathering. You can ask everyone to bring and share lunch or a picnic.

Anyone who feels they missed out on mothering when they were small can take their inner child to Cael for reassurance.

ZERACHIEL

Archangel for the sign of LEO
22 July – 21 August

ELEMENT Fire (yang)

PLANETARY ARCHANGEL Michael
  (the Sun)

SACRED STONES Ruby, cat's eye

SACRED GIFT A golden shield

QUALITY Fixed

KEYWORDS Glory, faith

COLOUR Orange

METAL Gold

MANIFESTATION Radiance,
  understanding

ABOUT ZERACHIEL

Zerachiel is a majestic, fiery archangel who works with the seraphim. He brings enthusiasm and vitality and illuminates the lives of all who meet him. His regal glory may seem overwhelming, but his spirit is generous and warm and his radiance brings hope into the world, especially on days when everything seems grey.

Like a benevolent father, Zerachiel enfolds you with a protective cloak of certainty and new courage. His tenacity will encourage you to go forwards even when you feel lost. He asks you to take charge of your life, to demonstrate your capacity to become sovereign of your inner self and develop nobility and generosity of spirit. He demands a high standard of integrity, reminding you to keep your heart open so that you recognise the divine spark in everyone you meet.

Zerachiel is the archangel for leaders of all kinds – Bill Clinton, Napoleon Bonaparte and Lawrence of Arabia are good examples. His splendid energy is also expressed by entertainers who give larger-than-life performances – think of Mick Jagger, Madonna and Geri Halliwell. But Zerachiel's energy can also be used to shine a light in dark places, and his generosity of spirit can offer humble service to others.

HOW ZERACHIEL CAN HELP YOU

Zerachiel works with Michael, Archangel of the Sun, to support positive leadership, generosity and courage. Ask Zerachiel for help if you:

❖ are feeling low in spirits and need to bring more spiritual sunshine into your life,
❖ need to take a leadership role in any situation,
❖ have to deal with a difficult or unreasonable person,
❖ want to encourage others to make the best of their lives, especially people who feel underprivileged or hopeless,
❖ want to make an inspiring speech or performance on stage in front of a large audience.

MEETING ZERACHIEL

Download the visualisation from www.workingwitharchangels.com, or pre-record and follow the instructions for the visualisation on pages 52–3, including the following words to speak to Zerachiel:

Archangel Zerachiel, let my heart beat with courage, so that I can illuminate the world with your sunshine.
Help me act from my sovereign self, meeting life's challenges with dignity and nobility.
Surround me with your radiant glory and remind me of your splendour every day.
Help me to provide positive leadership and encouragement to others and for the benefit of my community.

IDEAS FOR CONNECTING TO ZERACHIEL'S ENERGY

❖ Find a speech made by a famous leader and declare it out loud in the privacy of your own room – then find an opportunity to read it to other people.
❖ Get involved in a local committee and offer to be the chairperson.
❖ Look for a picture of a leader who inspires you personally and keep it by your desk, on your fridge or as a screen saver.

❖ Think about what frightens you most and imagine yourself being able to face that fear. You could write a story in which you are the hero or heroine and succeed in overcoming that fear.

❖ Invite your friends to a fancy dress party and ask them all to wear the most extravagant clothes they can find. Also ask them all to bring a bottle of the best champagne they can afford.

Zerachiel supports the noble virtues of loyalty, constancy and courage. He will be by your side whenever you need a champion to back your chosen cause, especially if it benefits a wide circle of people.

VAEL

Archangel for the sign of VIRGO
22 August – 21 September

ELEMENT Earth (yin)

PLANETARY ARCHANGEL The Shekinah – Charon (the moon of Pluto)

SACRED STONES Pink jasper, hyacinth

SACRED GIFT A girdle set with jasper

QUALITY Mutable

KEYWORDS Purity, service

COLOUR White

METAL Platinum

MANIFESTATION Discrimination, grace

ABOUT VAEL

Vael is the mysterious Lady of the Earth, mistress of devas and nature spirits. Her feet move silently in our world, but she is also crowned by shining stars. Her energy changes through the seasons: quiet under snow in winter, veiled with white blossoms in spring, abundant in summer and fruitful in autumn. She also works within the soul, summoning us to clear our inner channels so that we can be filled with divine grace.

When Vael calls us there are no sounding trumpets, just the quiet insistence that we must commit to clarity and discrimination. She asks us to serve the Divine by healing the land, working with nature spirits, providing for the needy and choosing only the highest possibilities for ourselves and others. She reminds us not to accept anything into our lives that is unworthy of our divine spirit.

Vael is efficient and modest and encourages us to work behind the scenes, offering our service without expectation of reward or recognition. Mother Teresa was a shining example of the humble, unglamorous commitment that brings remarkable results.

HOW VAEL CAN HELP YOU

Vael works well with the Shekinah, Archangel of Charon, the moon of Pluto. Her modest energy supports people who work with the earth or are in service to others. Ask Vael for help if you:

❖ are creating a new garden, especially one growing fruit, vegetables and herbs,

❖ work as a secretary or personal assistant, perhaps organising filing, or scheduling meetings for a busy boss,

❖ want to improve your efficiency: Vael will help you with clutter busting, since she likes everything to be precise and well organised,

❖ need to maintain a high standard of cleanliness – perhaps in a hospital or a kitchen,

❖ are learning a new skill that requires attention to detail.

MEETING VAEL

Download the visualisation from www.workingwitharchangels.com, or pre-record and follow the instructions for the visualisation on pages 52–3, including the following words to speak to Vael:

Archangel Vael, bring your quiet certainty into my soul and help me discriminate without being judgemental.

Help me to choose and serve the highest possibility, so that I am able to set standards and live up to them.

Open my awareness so that I can experience the hidden powers in nature, connecting with the invisible devas and nature spirits.

IDEAS FOR CONNECTING TO VAEL'S ENERGY

❖ Clear out your cupboards and drawers, and get new storage boxes and label them so that all your possessions have a place.

❖ Visit a herb garden, then plant some herbs for your own use, even if you only have a window box. Include herbs for both cooking and healing.

❖ Sort our your paperwork – your bills, letters, photographs. Set up a well-organised filing system.

❖ Offer your services to a local committee and take minutes of meetings. Or offer to make refreshments at a community event.

❖ Collect natural objects – leaves, berries, blossoms, seashells, pebbles – and make a nature table. Change the table each month to give you the feeling that you are connecting with the changing seasons.

❖ Donate to an organisation like Friends of the Earth or Trees for Life.

Vael encourages us to save and conserve, always making the best use of what is available. She works modestly in quiet places, often unnoticed, but she is effective and reliable – she will support you whenever you need to develop these qualities.

ZURIEL

Archangel for the sign of LIBRA
22 September – 22 October

ELEMENT Air (yang)

PLANETARY ARCHANGEL Raphael (Venus)

SACRED STONES Opal, amethyst

SACRED GIFT An opal scabbard

QUALITY Cardinal

KEYWORDS Beauty, harmony

COLOUR Lilac

METAL Copper

MANIFESTATION Balance, equilibrium

ABOUT ZURIEL

Zuriel initiates truth and wisdom wherever there is discord. He balances all the oppositions, light and dark, life and death, male and female. He understands both sides of every divine coin and weighs hearts and souls and minds on his silver scales. Even though Zuriel seems calm and a little detached he can act decisively – but only when all choices have been considered and weighed in the balance.

Zuriel encourages us to see the harmony and grace in all Creation, opening our eyes to the inner perfection of everything, despite outer conflicts. Through Zuriel we can gain understanding and direct knowledge of the divine laws governing our lives, and people who work with him are often seekers after justice. A good example is Archbishop Desmond Tutu, famous for his gentle but firm leadership in the United Nations, whose declared objective is 'a democratic and just society'. Eleanor Roosevelt, wife of the American President Roosevelt, worked constantly to improve the lot of the underprivileged everywhere and became one of the most revered women of her generation. Mahatma Gandhi, who challenged British rulership with non-violent opposition, is another shining example.

Because Zuriel encourages beauty and harmony we can work with him to create beautiful art, or to honour our own beauty. Elegance, good posture and exquisite design all come under Zuriel's remit.

HOW ZURIEL CAN HELP YOU

Zuriel works with Raphael, Archangel for Venus, helping you to adapt to change, and to actively seek divine guidance and inspiration. He helps people see both sides whenever there is a conflict of interest. Ask Zuriel for help if you:

❖ are trying to resolve a dispute of any kind,
❖ have to choose between two options that seem equally appealing,
❖ notice yourself becoming critical or judgemental,
❖ feel unable to speak out in defence of an underdog,
❖ want to improve your appearance,
❖ want to create more beauty or harmony in your home,
❖ want to heal an old emotional wound.

MEETING ZURIEL

Download the visualisation from www.workingwitharchangels.com, or pre-record and follow the instructions for the visualisation on pages 52–3, including the following words to speak to Zuriel:

Archangel Zuriel, let me walk the path of truth, justice and freedom.
Inspire me to speak words of divine law as I search for balance and harmony and never for retribution.
Allow me to bring beauty and grace into my life and all the lives that I touch daily.
Help me to stay centred and calm and to bring stillness and peace wherever I go.

IDEAS FOR CONNECTING TO ZURIEL'S ENERGY

❖ Become a mediator for a disadvantaged person – voluntary agencies welcome committed people who can speak up for someone with a poor education.
❖ Learn a game that requires an objective mind, such as chess.
❖ Take a class that encourages grace, good posture and serenity – such as yoga, Pilates or the Alexander Technique.
❖ Go to a law court to hear a case being argued.
❖ Support a group of people you feel are being unjustly treated – raise

funds, sign a petition, write letters to the press or join a rally that raises public awareness.

❖ Be an active citizen – attend local public meetings, or go to the Houses of Parliament to witness your representatives in action.

Zuriel supports any efforts we make to create and maintain balance, harmony and beauty.

BARUEL

Archangel for the sign of SCORPIO
23 October – 21 November

ELEMENT Water (yin)

PLANETARY ARCHANGEL Metatron
(Pluto)

SACRED STONES Topaz, malachite

SACRED GIFT A dagger jewelled
with topaz

QUALITY Fixed

KEYWORDS Justice, power

COLOUR Black

METAL Steel

MANIFESTATION
Determination, vigilance

ABOUT BARUEL

Baruel encourages us to explore the depths of consciousness and to uncover the mysteries of the universe. Her energy is like a coiled spring containing the power for dramatic transformation. She is mysterious, moving silently and secretly, carrying with her the knowledge of the metaphysical roots of Creation. She understands karmic processes and the many layers of the human soul, and brings solace to those in pain. She also bestows gifts of clairvoyance and intuition.

People who work with Baruel are disciplined, vigilant and resilient. With Baruel's help they are able to develop their psychic and paranormal abilities. They have enormous power and she helps them to understand how to temper it with wisdom and compassion – the hypnotist Paul McKenna uses his gifts to help people improve their lives. With Baruel's help they are able to develop their psychic and paranormal abilities. As well as the occult arts, empirical science also appeals to people born under Baruel's wings who want to uncover the secrets of the universe – famous physicists like Marie Curie, astronomers like Carl Sagan and Edmond Halley, and surgeons like Christian Barnard.

Baruel allows us to move between worlds unscathed, and her subjects always appear to have a sense of their own invincibility.

Whatever they do, it is done with passion – Sarah Bernhardt, Katharine Hepburn and Sylvia Plath all explored their art forms with great intensity.

HOW BARUEL CAN HELP YOU

Baruel has a powerful ally in Metatron, Archangel for Pluto, and together they can help you explore deeper reaches of reality. Ask Baruel for help if you:

❖ want to move your healing abilities to a new level,
❖ work in a hospice or are otherwise caring for someone who is dying,
❖ are learning any topic relating to the hidden structures of the universe, such as physics, astronomy or astrology,
❖ want to develop your intuition or paranormal powers.

MEETING BARUEL

Download the visualisation from www.workingwitharchangels.com, or pre-record and follow the instructions for the visualisation on pages 52–3, including the following words to speak to Baruel:

Archangel Baruel, help me access my true power and watch over me as I learn to use it wisely.
Allow me to access information from hidden dimensions of reality and guide me to use this knowledge for the benefit of all.
Use me as a channel to bring secret wisdom into the world when it is appropriate.
Help me to keep my counsel when I see things that will come to pass, but which cannot be changed.

IDEAS FOR CONNECTING TO BARUEL'S ENERGY

❖ Write your secret desires in your best handwriting on good-quality paper, roll it into a scroll, tie it with ribbon and hide it in a beautiful box.
❖ Learn a secret code, or script, so that you can write notes without anyone else being able to understand them.

❖ Develop healing skills, such as Reiki, or *shefa healing*, which direct life energy by using ancient symbols.

❖ Read books that describe human experiences after death – for example, the Egyptian or Tibetan *Book of the Dead*, past-life accounts, near-death experiences and so on.

❖ Consider what you would like to happen when you die – what you want to happen to your body and at your wake.

Baruel insists that we live life with passion and face death without fear.

ADNACHIEL

Archangel for the sign of SAGITTARIUS
22 November – 20 December

ELEMENT Fire (yang)

PLANETARY ARCHANGEL Zadkiel (Jupiter)

SACRED STONES Turquoise, lapis lazuli

SACRED GIFT A bow studded with lapis lazuli

QUALITY Mutable

KEYWORDS Wisdom, freedom

COLOUR Purple

METAL Tin

MANIFESTATION Philosophy, vision

ABOUT ADNACHIEL

Adnachiel calls us to far visions and distant lands. He brings inspiration into the hearts and souls of human beings, summoning them to seek divine wisdom. Like the other fiery archangels, Saraquael and Zerachiel, he is majestic and grand, and the mighty choirs of the seraphim surround him.

We are being summoned by Adnachiel to become wise counsellors, to encourage others to see the Divine in every grain of sand and to declare the glory of all Creation. With Adnachiel we can meet wise teachers who will guide us, or celestial beings that watch over our planet and protect the galaxies.

Adnachiel inspires us to prophesy, to learn from spiritual traditions and to declare our insights for the benefit of our fellows, always striving for the highest possibilities. The visionary poet and painter William Blake and the prophet Nostradamus both worked under Adnachiel's wings. Winston Churchill was a visionary who encouraged the British to see beyond their dark days to a new future. Beethoven was another of Adnachiel's protégés – his music transports us to higher realms.

In modern times Adnachiel inspires film-makers: Steven Spielberg and Walt Disney have both made films with uplifting and hopeful themes.

HOW ADNACHIEL CAN HELP YOU

Adnachiel works with Zadkiel to bring joy and inspiration into the world, encouraging us to shine light in dark places. Ask Adnachiel for help if you:

❖ want to meet an inner guide, perhaps a spiritual teacher from the past,

❖ want to bring hope and encouragement to anyone in despair,

❖ would like to create a ceremony or ritual for a life-cycle event or to celebrate the changing seasons,

❖ are raising funds for a charity that helps lonely or homeless people during the festive season,

❖ are composing a speech, or a piece of music, designed to encourage people to see light in a dark situation, or to raise their spiritual awareness,

❖ are seeking spiritual understanding in events that seem difficult or threatening.

MEETING ADNACHIEL

Download the visualisation from www.workingwitharchangels.com, or pre-record and follow the instructions for the visualisation on pages 52–3, including the following words to speak to Adnachiel:

Archangel Adnachiel, take me on a journey through celestial worlds, so that I can meet guides and teachers who will help me on my path.

Give me insight and wisdom, and fill me with divine energy so that I can live with enthusiasm every day.

Bring me opportunities to share messages of hope and freedom with people who feel oppressed by life.

Remind me to bring passion and commitment, tolerance and honesty into every aspect of my life.

IDEAS FOR CONNECTING TO ADNACHIEL'S ENERGY

❖ Be Santa Claus – collect gifts or organise a party for socially deprived children during the festive season.

❖ Listen to great classical music that stirs your soul – especially Beethoven.

❖ Create a ritual of thanksgiving for your life, utilising traditional symbols such as a chalice of wine and some bread, and using your own words.

❖ Write down your blessings to remind you of your connection to the Divine, in a few words that you can repeat on getting up and going to bed, or whenever you are in a difficult situation.

❖ Ride a bicycle down a hill, ride a horse across open fields – or undertake some other physical activity that gives you a sense of freedom.

Divine wisdom, freedom and generosity of spirit are the gifts of Adnachiel.

ORPHIEL

Archangel for the sign of CAPRICORN
21 December – 19 January

ELEMENT Earth (yin)

PLANETARY ARCHANGEL Samael
(Saturn)

SACRED STONES Jet, tourmaline

SACRED GIFT An antique casket

QUALITY Cardinal

KEYWORDS Reverence,
excellence

COLOUR Indigo

METAL Lead

MANIFESTATION Concentration,
worldly power

ABOUT ORPHIEL

Orphiel is a very practical archangel. Like the other archangels who rule earth signs, Ashmodiel (Taurus) and Vael (Virgo), she supports us individually and collectively as we try to create the best possible life on Earth. Orphiel helps us to set goals and create the structures that enable these goals to be realised. She is determined and powerful, focused and crisp, and totally dedicated to creating an earthly reality based on divine wisdom. She may seem stern, but do not underestimate her passion; she has a mother's tenacity and her intentions are based on timeless laws.

Just as every snowflake has a unique crystalline structure, so each human endeavour is based on invisible patterns that unfold through time until we reach the final result. Orphiel makes us aware of these underlying structures and the universal laws that will enable us to create heaven on Earth. This knowledge depends on divine authority, and our creative endeavours must be driven by our desire for the common good.

Orphiel asks us to use worldly power for heavenly purposes. Financiers like Howard Hughes and astute business people like Dolly Parton use Orphiel's energy. But people who focus their attention on justice for all, like Martin Luther King and Benjamin Franklin, bring higher inspiration to their practical aims. Although the mountain goat symbolising this sign suggests earthly climbing, the ancient image for Capricorn is a goat with a fish tail: Orphiel can take us to spiritual depths as well as worldly heights. The spiritual poet Kahlil Gibran was born under Orphiel's mantle.

HOW ORPHIEL CAN HELP YOU
Orphiel teams up with Samael to support us in our endeavours to improve life and make the best of our resources. Ask Orphiel for help if you:

❖ are planning anything, from a birthday party to building an extension to your house,
❖ are creating a business plan to present to your banker,
❖ are planning your career goals,
❖ are seeking appointment as a chair on a committee, as a local councillor or as parliamentarian,
❖ need to restructure your lifestyle in order to make the most of your time,
❖ have to deal with tax returns.

MEETING ORPHIEL
Download the visualisation from www.workingwitharchangels.com, or pre-record and follow the instructions for the visualisation on pages 52–3, including the following words to speak to Orphiel:

Archangel Orphiel, help me to be cautious, but not cold; prudent but not closed.
Teach me the hidden laws of Creation and direct me to use this knowledge with discrimination.
Help me achieve my ambitions with due consideration for other people's needs.
Remind me to be disciplined and show me how to use my will with kindness.

IDEAS FOR CONNECTING TO ORPHIEL'S ENERGY
❖ Keep a time-and-motion notebook for a week so that you know how you spend your time: could you allocate it better?

❖ Go to bed and get up earlier, and use the extra morning time to say blessings for the world and meditate, or to walk to work.

❖ Assess your spending habits for a week; set up a disciplined savings system.

❖ Do you have a pension plan, or another plan that will enable you to have a comfortable life in the future?

❖ Design an ideal plot for your life for the next five years and set goals for the coming year, month by month.

In order to work successfully with Orphiel, we need to be focused, discreet and determined. Discipline is necessary before we can find real freedom.

CAMBIEL

Archangel for the sign of AQUARIUS
20 January – 18 February

ELEMENT Air (yang)

PLANETARY ARCHANGEL Raziel
(Uranus)

SACRED STONES Sapphire,
blue topaz

SACRED GIFT A sapphire ring

QUALITY Fixed

KEYWORDS Truth,
investigation

COLOUR Electric blue

METAL Aluminium

MANIFESTATION Curiosity,
revolution

ABOUT CAMBIEL

Cambiel's energy reminds us of the stillness of the upper air, high above the clouds. He soars like an eagle, watching the grandeur of the world from a place of calm and equanimity. This archangel sees above, below and beyond, and showers us with inspiration, grace and blessings.

When we work with Cambiel we are privileged to understand the unity of divine Creation and how divine laws apply to all. Cambiel encourages us to seek the truth and to be guided by traditional values, but also to be prepared to overturn outmoded rules and regulations. People who work with Cambiel often have an inspired capacity to access knowledge, creativity or sudden flashes of inspiration: Mozart said he simply wrote down what he heard, as though he was channelling the music of the spheres; the engineer Emmanuel Swedenborg visited heaven and conversed with angels.

People ruled by Cambiel have ideas that may seem out of step with those of their peers, and they rarely join groups. Charles Darwin developed the theory of evolution that challenged the thinking of his day; Galileo overturned the medieval view of cosmology. The artist Jackson Pollock gave up brushes and threw paint on his canvas. Germaine Greer encouraged women to take up their rights in the workplace. Derren Brown has cast a new light on exploring the power of the mind.

HOW CAMBIEL CAN HELP YOU

Cambiel works with Raziel to open our consciousness to higher realms and offers us access to divine wisdom. Ask Cambiel to help if you:

❖ feel the need to stand up for equal rights in any situation,
❖ are working on a creative project that would benefit from a new approach,
❖ want to make an effective contribution to your community, without necessarily joining an organisation,
❖ would like to encourage people you know to rethink their attitudes or lifestyle.

MEETING CAMBIEL

Download the visualisation from www.workingwitharchangels.com, or pre-record and follow the instructions for the visualisation on pages 52–3, including the following words to speak to Cambiel:

Archangel Cambiel, take me to the airy heights, so that I can view Creation and see the equality of all creatures.
Allow me to channel new insights that will help humanity on its journey of self-discovery.
Help me to understand and reveal to others the mysteries of Creation, so that everyone can feel their connection to the divine source.
Inspire me to encourage people to share resources and treat all God's creatures with respect.

IDEAS FOR CONNECTING TO CAMBIEL'S ENERGY

❖ Offer support to someone who is despised – for example, visit or write to a prisoner.
❖ Involve yourself in local activities, with the aim of improving the lot of people who have to live in a run-down area.
❖ Explore human rights by researching on the Internet, so that you understand what is going on today and who is working to improve the status of minorities.
❖ Try out a schoolchild's science kit – perhaps using magnets or growing crystals.

❖ Visit a planetarium and gaze at the stars, planets and galaxies: think about how small we are, but also how amazing we are.

❖ Read a book that helps the lay person to understand quantum physics.

Not only can Cambiel help us to understand the mysteries of the universe, but in order to live up to his expectations we must also be motivated by ideals of liberty, equality and justice.

BARAKIEL

Archangel for the sign of PISCES
19 February – 20 March

ELEMENT Water (yin)	QUALITY Mutable
PLANETARY ARCHANGEL Zaphkiel (Neptune)	KEYWORDS Love, unity
	COLOUR Rise pink
SACRED STONES Rose quartz, moonstone	METAL Platinum
	MANIFESTATION Insight,
SACRED GIFT Seashell slippers	clairvoyance

ABOUT BARAKIEL

Barakiel brings us wisdom from the deep ocean of the collective consciousness of humanity, and reconnects our spiritual cords to the source of divine compassion. She is a loving mother who moves gentle tides of healing water across your soul. She shimmers like a mermaid, bringing wordless knowledge from beyond the edge of time. She breathes softly in the heart of the Divine, bringing love towards her, and then releasing it to us. Her love moves in our hearts like a rose or a lotus unfolding its soft petals.

When we work with Barakiel, the barriers to love melt away and we realise how close we are to heaven. We understand that our own souls are timeless and immortal, that there is no death, only the infinite and endless life-giving power of God. She asks you to surrender to divine love and to give ceaselessly so that she can fill you over and over again

Barakiel's gifts include clairvoyance and insight – both Rudolf Steiner and Edgar Cayce, the 'sleeping prophet', were under Barakiel's care. Her mystical beauty is expressed in film, dance and theatre: the ballet dancer Rudolf Nureyev was often compared to the earlier dancer Nijinsky – they were both born under this sign – and the actress Elizabeth Taylor, also born under Barakiel's sign, was nicknamed 'Ocean' by her partner Richard Burton.

HOW BARAKIEL CAN HELP YOU

Barakiel works with Zaphkiel to remind us that all we need is love, and that loving is easier than carrying anger and resentment. Ask Barakiel for help if you:

❖ find it difficult to forgive someone or to say sorry,
❖ want to develop your clairvoyant gifts,
❖ would like to express your spiritual insights in the form of poetry or music,
❖ have low self-esteem and feel unworthy of love,
❖ are mourning the death of a loved one,
❖ are afraid of your own death.

MEETING BARAKIEL

Download the visualisation from www.workingwitharchangels.com, or pre-record and follow the instructions for the visualisation on pages 52–3, including the following words to speak to Barakiel:

Archangel Barakiel, fill me with divine love, so that I can give uncon-ditionally.
Bring me dreams and visions that will help me experience other dimen-sions.
Help me inspire others to experience your loving tenderness.
Let me see beyond death and receive direct understanding of the unity of all Creation.

IDEAS FOR CONNECTING TO BARAKIEL'S ENERGY

❖ If possible, visit a seaside place where you can see live dolphins – or watch a DVD about dolphins.
❖ Buy yourself a big bunch of pink roses or use rose essence as perfume.
❖ Swim in the sea, or buy some Dead Sea salts for your bath.
❖ Find a picture or statuette of a mermaid to keep in your room.
❖ Make a scented foam bath and while you are soaking, visualise being taken on a seashell chariot to a magical water kingdom where the undines nurture you and give you messages of love for yourself and people you know.

❖ Listen to classical piano music. Chopin was born under this sign and his music will transport you to higher realms.

❖ Bless everyone you see for a whole day, regardless of your opinion of their worthiness.

❖ Join a group for regular meditations and send out blessings to the world.

❖ Light candles for loved ones who have died.

With Barakiel there is no fear for the future, no regret for the past; she heals hurts and washes away old wounds.

Your Dream Team

Now that you have read about the archangels who can help humanity both individually and collectively, you have the opportunity to improve your life and bring more joy and happiness to others. You can use this book to remind you of the powerful inner helpers who are at hand whenever you need to call on their resources, whether for courage, determination, healing, tenderness or any of the other qualities that the archangels represent. You could think of them as your Cabinet ministers or councillors, each of whom has a particular remit.

One way to work effectively with the archangels is to choose your 'Dream Team', a small group of archangels selected for the specific qualities you need to work with at a particular time in your life. An essential member of your Dream Team is your Guardian Angel, who must always be included. I also suggest you include the zodiac archangel for your Sun sign. In addition to these two assistants, select between two and four additional archangels as a task force to support your goals, which must be carefully defined. For example, writing this book that has meant sitting at a computer for a few hours a day and I feel I need to increase my physical activities. I want to increase my stamina and lose some weight, but it is winter, and I am feeling very lazy! So, for my Dream Team I would choose:

❖ My Guardian Angel.
❖ My Sun sign archangel, Saraquael, for the sign of Aries, to give me vitality.

- ❖ Hanael, because he works well with Saraquael and I need that extra yang energy.
- ❖ Samael, because she will insist on self-discipline.
- ❖ Ashmodiel, Archangel for Taurus. She helps anyone wishing to improve the state of their body and will boost my determination.

Think about what is going on for you at present, consider what kind of help you need and choose your own Dream Team. How long you work with your chosen team will depend on your goals. Put a timeframe in place. For example, you might want to increase your income over the next three months. With a clear goal and a deadline, you will be able to measure your success. If you aren't getting results, change your team!

A few weeks or months down the line, you may get a strong feeling that the issues you were addressing have mostly been resolved, but that something else is looming. In this case revisit your chosen team and see who needs to be fired or hired to create a suitable new Dream Team.

If you prefer, you can always work with just one archangel at a time. And don't forget that you can turn to the archangels at any time and anywhere. They reside deep in the hidden dimensions of our collective consciousness, an infinite resource for humanity, willing to work with us as we strive to heal ourselves and our world. Within our hearts we know that we have the divine capacity to create heaven on Earth, and the archangels will always support our commitment to make this happen.

Appendix 1: Meditation

I encourage my students to use a mantra for their meditation – a specific sound repeated silently within the mind. The mantra enables your thoughts to settle into a quieter pattern, which allows your consciousness to expand. Instead of thinking about everyday pre-occupations, you will find that you are able to listen to guidance from the depths of your own being. This will allow you to receive clear messages from angels and archangels, and possibly from other guides and invisible spiritual helpers.

Mantras are usually chosen from a sacred language, such as Sanskrit or Hebrew. Many of the sounds in these languages have helpful vibrations, which connect us to the powerful creative forces in the universe. I recommend using the word *shalom* – Hebrew for 'peace' – because it has three powerful sounds in it:[61]

Sssh – the sound of universal energy,
Aah – for creative intention,
and Ommm – for manifestation.

Try introducing the word *shalom* into your meditation. On the first occasion, you can say it out loud a few times, then gradually say it more quietly, until eventually you are just repeating it in your head.

Sit quietly for 20 minutes and just allow the word *shalom* to come and go in your mind. Do not force it. Contrary to popular belief, you do not need to concentrate hard on the mantra. If other thoughts come into your mind, as they will, do not become anxious, just notice the other thoughts and then, when you notice that you have forgotten the mantra, go back to it. It's easy. Your body will become still, your breathing will naturally become slower and deeper. Your thoughts will gradually quieten down and you will be filled with peace and light.

One misunderstanding about meditation is to assume that you should *not* think. It is natural for thoughts to arise in the mind, and when we allow the mind a free space then we find that creative thoughts, inspiration and wisdom come easily to us.

Appendix 2: Recommendations

Books

Astell, Chrissie, *Advice from Angels,* London: Godsfield Press, 2005

Bach, Edward, *The Twelve Healers* (pamphlet), Saffron Walden, Essex: C.W. Daniel Co. Ltd, 1983

Bialik, H. and Ravnitzky, Y., trans., Braude, W., *The Book of Legends (The Aggadah)*, New York: Schocken Press, 1988

Cohn-Sherbok, Dan, *Jewish Mysticism – an anthology*, Oxford: OneWorld, 1995

Cortens, Theolyn, *Living with Angels,* London: Piatkus, 2003

Cortens, Theolyn, *Working with Your Guardian Angel*, London: Piatkus, 2005

Cortens, Theolyn, *The Angels' Script*, London: SoulSchool, 2004

Dan, Joseph, ed., *The Heart and the Fountain*, Oxford: Oxford University Press, 2002

d'Angelo, Ishvara, *Angels in our Time*, O Books, 2006

Davidson, Gustav, *Dictionary of Angels*, New York: Simon & Schuster, 1994

Fortune, Dion, *The Mystical Qabalah*, Wellingborough, Northants: Aquarian Press, 1987

Gikatilla, Joseph, trans., Weinstein, Avi, *The Gates of Light*, San Francisco: Harper Collins, 1994

Ginzberg, Louis, ed., Radin, Paul, trans., *Legends of the Jews*, London: John Hopkins Press Ltd, 1998

Godwin, Malcolm, *Angels: an Endangered Species*, London: Boxtree, 1993

Guilley, Rosemary Ellen, *Angels of Mercy*, New York: Simon and Schuster Pocket Books, 1994

Hall, Judy, *The Crystal Bible*, London: Godsfield Press, 2003

Halevi, Z'ev ben Shimon, *Tree of Life*, London: Rider (1972), 1983

Kaplan, Aryeh, trans., *The Bahir*, York Beach, Maine: Samuel Weiser, 1989

Kaplan, Aryeh, trans., *The Sefer Yetzirah*, York Beach, Maine: Samuel Weiser, 1997

Mafi, Maryam, and Kolin, Azima Melita, trans., *Rumi, Hidden Music*, London: Thorsons Element, 2001

Parisen, Maria, ed., *Angels and Mortals: Their Co-creative Power*, London: Quest Books, 1990

Pepper, Kathleen, *Essential Oils and Meditation*, London: Polair Publishing, 2007

Porter, J.R., *The Lost Bible*, London: Duncan Baird Publishers, 2001

Rosen, Jeremy, *Kabbalah Inspirations*, London: Duncan Baird Publishers, 2005

Tishby, Isaiah, trans., *The Wisdom of the Zohar*, Portland, Oregon: Litmann Jewish Library, 2002

Wilson, Peter Lamborn, *Angels*, London: Thames and Hudson, 1980

Music

Your choices of music will be very personal. A lot of New Age music designed for angel meditation provides general, healing ambient sound, which is very suitable for healing and for creating that gentle quality we associate with angelic support.

However, I advise you to experiment with some of the great classics and discover for yourself whose music seems to resonate with the qualities of the archangel you are working with. Since each archangel creates a different kind of energetic field, this will be reflected in the art, music and poetry manifested by creative artists, composers and writers. Invariably, each creative person will express a quality that can be identified with the archangels associated with his or her zodiac sign, and the Tree of Life archangel who connects with it. Take, for example, the calm, balanced paintings of the Italian artist Canaletto, whose serene pictures of Venice and London reflect the fact that he was born under the wings of Zuriel, archangel for the sign of Libra, whose Tree of Life archangel is Raphael. Now think of the difference between the passionate music of Beethoven (Adnachiel: Sagittarius and Zadkiel), and the delicate, soothing piano compositions of Chopin (Barakiel: Pisces and Zaphkiel). These great composers were expressing the energetic qualities of the archangels who worked with them.

You don't need to know the composer's birth date – just choose by sensing the effect the sounds have on you.

Websites

www.workingwitharchangels.com

The website specially created for readers of this book. Download visualisations read by Theolyn, and view images and other helpful material.

www.alisterhardyreligiousexperience.co.uk

Based at the University of Wales, this organisation, founded by an Oxford professor, supports research into all kinds of spiritual experiences, including angels and near-death experience. It offers conferences and residential weekends with a variety of speakers. I usually attend these and often speak myself. Membership of the society is very reasonable.

www.angelart.me.uk

Angel painter and author Ishvara d'Angelo.

www.angellight.co.uk

Angel teacher and author Chrissie Astell.

www.angelwingstrading.net

Valentia Lythrin, a qualified SoulSchool teacher, has developed a wonderful set of archangel essences, based on her work with the Tree of Life archangels. A set of these would be an invaluable support for anyone working with the archangels in this book.

www.cygnus_books.co.uk

Excellent book club offering well-priced Mind, Body and Spirit books and free magazine.

www.keystolight.co.uk

Kathleen Pepper, yoga and crystal teacher.

www.thepsychichighway.com

Resource for information about all matters related to Mind, Body and Spirit. Members can exchange news and views, upload their events, and get discounts on books, courses and events.

www.shefahealing.org

For information about this remarkable new healing technique, based on ancient celestial symbols, with dates of upcoming courses.

www.soulschool.co.uk

Theolyn's teaching organisation, offering workshops and home-study courses. Find dates of events organised by Theolyn and SoulSchool teachers.

www.spiritualitywales.co.uk

Hagia Sofia interfaith chapel in Wales.

www.theolyn.com

For current information about Theolyn's poetry and other creative rojects.

www.visionaryliving.com

Rosemary Ellen Guiley, angel researcher.

Please see the SoulSchool website for links to individual teachers' websites

SoulSchool

SOULSCHOOL is Theolyn's teaching organisation, offering workshops, classes, home-study courses and Shefa Healing. These workshops are available in the UK, but Theolyn and SoulSchool qualified teachers also travel to fulfil requests for international events.

- ❖ **Messages from Angels** One-day workshops learning to use *The Angels' Script* cards, with angelic messages channelled by Theolyn.
- ❖ **Working with your Guardian Angel** A series of evening classes, weekly or fortnightly, based on Theolyn's book of the same name, published by Piatkus.
- ❖ **Working with Archangels** Monthly one-day workshops, designed to cover the twelve archangels in this book.
- ❖ **Shefa Healing** A two-day non-residential training course. After an additional period of on-going practice and contact with your teacher, you can qualify to give Shefa Healing professionally.

❖ **Discovering Angels** Three-month home-study course, occasionally available as a fast-track five-day retreat.

❖ **Paths to Transformation** Nine-month home-study course, working with the archangels and the symbols from *The Angels' Script* to accelerate your spiritual development.

❖ **Diploma in Teaching, Healing and Spiritual Coaching** Nine-month course for anyone wishing to become a SoulSchool teacher.

Also available through SoulSchool

Living with Angels	Theolyn's excellent book for beginners gives lots of practical advice for bringing angels into your everyday life. A great classic book for your collection.
Working with Your Guardian Angel	This 12-week course book will help you discover your life purpose and develop a practical relationship with your divine life coach.
The Angels' Script	Full-colour set of 36 cards, including cards for the Archangels of the Tree of Life and angelic symbols. Illustrated book with sample spreads. You can try out a reading at www.soulschool.co.uk.
Working with Archangels CD	All the visualisations from this book.
Living with Angels CD	All the visualisations from *Living with Angels* – and some added extras!
Quick and Easy Meditation CD	A practical starter for meditating with a mantra.
Archangel Essences	Created by Valentia Lithryn.

For details see www.soulschool.co.uk or telephone for a prospectus on 0845 458 0628 or +44 (0) 208 341 6792.

Endnotes

1 The popular modern version of Kabbalah has been adapted from this ancient, secret tradition.

2 The oldest carving of a winged being I have come across was found in Iraq and dates back to 1000 BC. This bas-relief image, carved in basalt, is about two feet high and depicts a figure with three pairs of wings, holding a snake in each hand.

3 The date and authorship of this book is uncertain.

4 The Book of Tobit is found in the *Apocrypha*, which contains scriptures excluded from the main body of the Bible. Again the dates of this book are uncertain; some scholars date it as early as the 8th century BC, others to the 2nd century BC.

5 Also included in the *Apocrypha*, probably written around the 1st century.

6 Pseudo-Dionysius was called 'pseudo' because he used a pseudonym, concealing his true identity. He claimed that his information about celestial realms came from a disciple of St Paul called Dionysius who had lived about 500 years earlier. Many theologians of his time distrusted his teachings on angels, but others accepted his work as genuine mystical insights.

7 Mesopotamia was the name for a long strip of land between the rivers Euphrates and Tigris, with Assyria in the north and Babylonia in the south. Mesopotamia literally means 'between the rivers'. This area of land roughly equates to present day Iraq.

8 See Shefa Healing, p. 234.

9 In other non-biblical texts, such as *Jubilees*, the evil one is called Belial. Beliar may mean 'without light'.

10 Israel Regardie (1907–85) was briefly secretary to another member of the Golden Dawn, the infamous Aleister Crowley (1875–1947) who is reputed to have practised black magic. Regardie avoided the scandal associated with Crowley and became well known as an effective chiropractor.

11 *The Middle Pillar*, first published in 1938.

12 Qabalah is an older spelling for Kabbalah.

13 Elizabeth Clare Prophet also claimed to receive messages from 'ascended masters', spiritual teachers who support the development of higher consciousness in humanity. The masters were introduced to the West by Madame Blavatsky, who founded the Theosophical Society in 1875.

   The term 'ascended master' comes from the occult tradition and refers to people who have become adepts by developing their magical abilities and acquiring paranormal skills, such as levitation, bi-location and longevity. They are not to be confused with past saints, prophets or other spiritual teachers whose focus was on their relationship with the divine source rather than on overcoming the limitations of the material world.

14 Aldous Huxley: *The Doors of Perception*, 1954. The title comes from William Blake's *Marriage of Heaven and Hell* (1793): 'If the doors of perception were cleansed, everything would appear to man as it is: infinite/For man has closed himself up, till he sees all things thro' narrow chinks of his cavern.'

15 Founded in the 1960s by Sir Alister Hardy, Professor of Marine Biology at Oxford University, who invited members of the public to write in with their spiritual experiences.

16 Meg Maxwell and Vera Tschudin (eds), *Seeing the Invisible*, p. 112, 1996, RERC Oxford (Alister Hardy Archive 2067).

17 In 1996 John Travolta played Michael in a film of the same name. In the film, Michael was rather overweight and put a great deal of sugar on his cornflakes, but whenever he got the chance he would take off his overcoat and shout 'Battle!'

18 Mother Teresa would have said that her mission was based on her love of Jesus and his mother, Mary. But the loving qualities we associate with Jesus and Mary are also those of Zaphkiel.

19 On the website www.workingwitharchangels.com you will find a beautiful chant invoking the four best-known archangels: Michael, Gabriel, Raphael and Auriel. I use it at the beginning of my workshops. Nickomo, who created it, has given me permission to make it freely available, so you can download it and use it at the beginning of your sessions, if you wish.

20 For information about Shefa Healing, see Appendix p. 234.

21 The spiritually ambitious rabbi eventually overreached himself and came to a sticky end. The full story is told in Joseph Dan (ed.), *The Heart and the Fountain*, OUP, 2003.

22 Another book that has been excluded from the Hebrew and Christian Bibles. This 'lost book' dates to about the end of the 1st century AD.

23 This is one of the texts mentioned earlier which are not included in the Hebrew or Christian Bibles.

24 The Book of Esdras is included in the *Apocrypha*, which is included in Roman Catholic Bibles, but not in most Protestant versions.

25 *See* Dion Fortune, *The Mystical Qabalah*, Wellingborough, Northants: Aquarian Press, 1987.

26 Other names for angels do appear in the Hebrew Bible: in the Book of Genesis the guiding angel of Israel is called Beth-El (Genesis 31.11–13). In *Hosea*, Beth-El is referred to both as *malakh* (angel) and *elohim*; in Hebrew the word *elohim* is the plural of *el*, meaning God – literally 'the shining ones' – and does not indicate gender.

27 In St Mark's version of the Resurrection, the angel who meets the two Marys at the tomb of Jesus is described as a young man wearing a long white garment (Mark 16.5).

28 In the *Midrash Tanhuma*, a collection of stories that dates back to the 8th century AD.

29 See *The Angels' Script* first published 1997, 2nd edition 2000, SoulSchool Publishing, London.

30 Gustav Davidson, *A Dictionary of Angels*, New York: Simon & Schuster, 1994.

31 But other sources, such as Francis Barrett's *The Magus* (first published London, 1801), put Chamuel in place of Samael.

32 From the Jewish *Aggadah*.

33 The *Torah* consists of the first five books of the Bible, also called the Books of Moses. In the Christian Church they are called the Pentateuch – *penta* means five.

34 Freake, trans., Tyson, ed., Agrippa, *Three Books of Occult Philosophy*, Llewellyn Publications, St Paul Mn 1993.

35 See the chapter on Metatron, p. 149.

36 Dylan Thomas, 'The force that through the green fuse drives the flower'.

37 Ingrid Bergman played Gladys in the 1958 film of her story, called *The Inn of the Sixth Happiness*.

38 Solomon's ring with the five-pointed star is not to be confused with 'Solomon's Seal', which is a six-pointed star, sometimes called the Star, or Shield, of David. King David was Solomon's father.

39 The apple has traditionally been sacred to Venus. If you cut an apple laterally across the middle the pips form a pattern like a five-pointed star.

40 The Book of Tobit is an 'apocryphal' book, included in the Catholic Bible, but not in the Hebrew or Protestant Bibles.

41 Many Jews were taken into captivity from their homeland to Assyria in the latter part of the 8th century BC.

42 This story has been illustrated by many artists through the century. Recently the author Salley Vickers incorporated the story of Tobias into her novel *Miss Garnet's Angel*, Penguin Books, London, 2001.

43 Gustav Davidson, *A Dictionary of Angels*, New York: Simon & Schuster, 1994.

44 Probably composed *c*. 1–2nd century AD.

45 See p. 72.

46 W. E. Henley 1849–1903.

47 Thomas Traherne, *Centuries of Meditation*, 1.29.

48 In the kabbalistic tradition it is said that there are thirty-six *zeddikim* – righteous people – living on our planet at any one time.

49 There is a statue of Melchizedek carrying initiatory gifts of bread and wine on the front of Chartres Cathedral.

50 Z'ev ben Shimon Halevi, *Tree of Life*, London, Rider (1972), 1983, p. 63.

51 C.S. Lewis, *The Lion, the Witch and the Wardrobe*, 1950.

52 John Bunyan, *The Pilgrim's Progress*, 1678.

53 Astrology does not tell you your future because you have free will, but it can show you your 'hand of cards' – the possibilities you have to work with.

54 Literal ascension to heaven is a rare event in biblical stories – it happened to Enoch, to Elijah and to Jesus. The term 'ascended master' comes from the occult tradition; see Endnote 13.

55 Written between the 7th and 9th centuries.

56 Gustav Davidson in his *Dictionary of Angels* suggests that the Shekinah is comparable to Shakti, the Hindu divine mother that is the bride of the god Shiva.

57 From 'The Account of Creation' in the *Zohar*.

58 Louis Untermeyer, ed., New York, Simon and Schuster, 1942.

59 See www.spiritualitywales.co.uk

60 But remember to keep grounded by also working with Ashmodiel (p. 182), Orphiel (p. 244) or Vael (p. 198).

61 My *Quick and Easy Meditation* CD gives clear instructions and guides you through learning the mantra meditation. You can use this CD to start your process, and then work on your own when you feel confident.

Index